Beauty from Ashes

An Eyewitness Account of Haiti's Tragic Earthquake

Melanie Wright Zeeb

AMBASSADOR INTERNATIONAL
GREENVILLE, SOUTH CAROLINA & BELFAST, NORTHERN IRELAND

www.ambassador-international.com

Beauty From Ashes

An Eyewitness Account of Haiti's Tragic Earthquake

ISBN: 978-1-62020-262-3
eISBN: 978-1-62020-363-7

Cover Design by Hannah Nichols
Page Layout by Joshua Frederick
eBook Conversion by Anna Riebe

AMBASSADOR INTERNATIONAL
Emerald House
427 Wade Hampton Blvd.
Greenville, SC 29609, USA
www.ambassador-international.com

AMBASSADOR BOOKS
The Mount
2 Woodstock Link
Belfast, BT6 8DD, Northern Ireland, UK
www.ambassador-international.com

The colophon is a trademark of Ambassador

DEDICATION

For the children who lived this story
And the families who call them their own.

ACKNOWLEDGEMENTS

Thank you to my parents, Dale and Joyce Wright, who allowed me the time and space to heal when I moved home from Haiti. Your love and support throughout my life have been invaluable.

Thank you to my husband, Matt, who married me in the middle of this crazy writing process and has supported me through it, even when he didn't always understand it.

Thank you to my mom and to Susan, who read through many drafts of this book, offering advice and encouragement as needed, and without whom this book might never have been completed.

Thank you to all the families whose stories are told in this book. I am honored that you entrusted your stories to me, and I know that this book is better because of them. I am even more honored that I was entrusted with your children when they and I were at GLA. My life is richer from knowing them and I am thankful that I was introduced to you through your amazing children.

Thank you to Joel Trimble, Joe and Jill Wilkins, and Bas Spuybroek, who shared their photographs and video footage with me, allowing me to experience parts of the journey that I was not present for.

Thank you to the publishing team at Ambassador International for believing in this story and giving it the opportunity to go out into the world, and to my copyeditor, JP Brooks, for making it a stronger story than I ever could have done alone.

Thank you to my heavenly Father, who has given me a life beyond any I could have imagined. You answered the long-forgotten prayers of this little girl who wanted to live adventures and write a part of your story. I am blessed.

CONTENTS

INTRODUCTION

HAITI WAS NEVER PART OF my life plan. If living overseas was ever something I considered, it involved going to one of the many countries where they speak English, or at least Spanish, which I had studied for several years.

In spite of these and other objections, in June 2004 I ended up on a mission trip to Haiti with the church I was attending at the time. This trip changed me, how I viewed the world, and the entire course of the next several years of my life.

To be honest, I did not immediately love Haiti. In fact, by the end of the first day, I hated it. From the moment our plane landed that afternoon, I was assaulted by unfamiliar smells and sights: burning trash, crowded city streets, brightly painted trucks crammed with people, rough roads, nearly-naked children, and tiny shacks that served as homes. I felt like I had stepped into a National Geographic video, and I didn't know how to reconcile what I was experiencing with the world I had always known. Perhaps I didn't actually hate Haiti so much as I felt overwhelmed by it, but I was miles outside my comfort zone and I didn't like it.

By the next day, my attitude had begun to change as I started meeting the Haitian people. I had seen their poverty the day before, but now I saw them for the people they were. They had hopes and dreams and a resilience I would not have imagined. I was already beginning to love and admire these people, and I quickly realized that the only difference between us that mattered was where we were born. If I had been born in Haiti, my situation would be the same as that of these people I had come to serve. I had done nothing to deserve being born in the United States, with all its wealth and opportunity. By the end of the week, I had wrestled with these truths and, though I had by no means found all the answers, my experiences had touched me in such a way that I already knew I must come back.

So I returned the following year, spending six months teaching English in an orphanage. In 2007, I spent another two months in Haiti, teaching and volunteering at a different orphanage. Throughout those years, I also went on as many weeklong mission trips back to Haiti as possible. Every time my plane landed on Haitian soil, I felt like I was coming home.

Finally, I found what I had been searching for: an opportunity to live and work in Haiti on a long-term basis. I was offered a job at an orphanage named "God's Littlest Angels." GLA had begun thirteen years earlier with saving the life of one tiny premature baby, but it had since become a large orphanage that processed dozens of international adoptions each year. In addition to the Bickel family—John and Dixie (who directed GLA) and their adult daughter Laurie—seven other staff members from the United States, Canada, and Scotland worked at GLA performing a variety of duties. There were also more than eighty Haitians employed to care for the children, staff, and visitors: office staff, drivers, nannies, nurses, schoolteachers, cooks, housekeepers, and laundry ladies.

I moved to Haiti in April 2008 to join the staff of GLA as their update coordinator. This meant I would be responsible for taking pictures of all the children each month and sending them, along with anecdotes about the children and their growth, to their adoptive families around the world. Best of all, I would get to spend time with the children.

By the start of 2010, as I was nearing the completion of my second year in Haiti, GLA rented three properties located within half a mile of one another in the neighborhood of Thomassin 32. The main house was home to the youngest children, from birth to approximately two years of age. It typically housed around ninety children, in addition to the Bickel family's apartment and the main offices. Several long-term staff members lived in a separate apartment-style building adjacent to the main house. The toddler house was located within easy walking or driving distance up the mountain. It was where the older children, ages three to thirteen, lived in separate buildings for the boys and the girls. Besides the sixty children and the toddler house staff living there, short-term volunteers stayed in dorm rooms at the toddler house during their time at GLA. The newest rental property was the guesthouse, which was located a few houses up the road from the toddler house. Visiting families whose adoptions were complete or who were required to come to Haiti to file paperwork stayed in the guesthouse.

This was the world that had become my life.

PART I

EARTHQUAKE
AND AFTERMATH

CHAPTER 1

7.0

God is our refuge and strength,
an ever-present help in trouble.
Therefore we will not fear, though the earth give way
and the mountains fall into the heart of the sea.

~ Psalm 46:1–2

JANUARY 12, 2010

THE SUN ROSE OVER THE mountains in the east, its rays brightening the early morning hours. The beauty of those mountains, the nearby sea, and the clear blue sky were largely unnoticed, hidden as they were by people's busyness, the less grand surroundings of their immediate environs, or simply by their familiarity. It was the unobtrusive start of a new day in Haiti, but it was a day that would never be forgotten.

As yet, the people were unaware of what the coming hours would bring. They saw simply the start of a new day with the same challenges as yesterday. They headed to work, to school, to the market—the activities that made up their daily lives and routine. The good-byes to family and neighbors, so casually spoken, would soon take on a much greater significance.

A few miles outside the capital city of Port-au-Prince, about halfway up the mountain between Petionville and Kenscoff, I was starting my day at God's Littlest Angels. I began work earlier than usual, my duties for the day requiring the early start. I was also eager to make up for the time I had lost the previous week when my luggage, including the studio backdrop I needed for photographing the children, didn't arrive at the same time I did, after my return from spending Christmas with my family in Indiana.

The mountain air was cool in the early morning, especially for those of us used to Haiti's tropical climate. Visitors from North America and Europe would laugh to see us wearing long sleeves in such pleasant and mild weather. There had been a time when I agreed with them, but I had thoroughly acclimated to Haiti's climate, and that Tuesday morning I wore a sweatshirt over my shorts and t-shirt.

My job for the day was to finish photographing our children for the monthly updates I would send out in a few weeks. I had spent the previous day taking pictures of the first half of the children at the main house; the toddler house photos had been completed late the previous week. It was a physically and mentally demanding job: lifting children up and down off the large table which served as a platform, bending over and moving to get the right angle for whichever direction the child was inclined to look, and coaxing smiles out of the children who, in spite of the regularity of this process, often seemed confused and perplexed by what was going on. The volunteers worked with me: retrieving children from their nurseries, dressing them up for their photographs, then changing them back into their nursery clothes and taking them downstairs again when they were done. The morning passed uneventfully and, though I was unable to take all the children's photos during the morning hours, when it was time to take a break for lunch, I was confident I would be able to finish in the afternoon.

When I went downstairs at noon, I learned that the others' day had not been going well. We were always busy at GLA, and it was often stressful working for an orphanage that processed adoptions and cared for more than 150 children at two separate houses. Minor, or often more than minor, obstacles were a normal part of life in Haiti. The Caribbean nation is one of contradictions: beauty and pain, rich and poor, hope and despair, joy and suffering. Haiti is a place with its own unique culture, but it is one that is often quite puzzling for those of us with a Western mindset. Things do not work in the ways that seem logical to us, nor do they happen on our schedule. Luxuries such as running water and electricity, if available at all, are unreliable. Time schedules are much more relaxed than we are used to, and things happen when people get around to them, which is rarely at our earliest convenience. A minor wiring or plumbing problem, for example, could take days or weeks to resolve. Many of our biggest frustrations came from our work in the realm of international adoptions. Computers were nearly non-existent in Haitian government offices, so most processing of adoptions was done by hand. We often struggled with the delays and setbacks of misplaced papers, files on the bottom of ever-growing stacks of paperwork, and the occasional disappearance of important legal documents that had to be replaced. Each delay was frustrating on its own, but these delays were made worse by the fact that each file represented a child whose time in the orphanage was prolonged while he waited to join his adoptive family.

That second Tuesday in January was one of those days when all the frustrations seemed to be coming at once. Long, pointless phone calls, annoying decisions by adoption officials, and papers that could not be found were among the nuisances of the morning for our office staff. Laurie's computer had unexpectedly crashed over the weekend, leaving her information inaccessible and making her work as GLA's accountant much more difficult. In the nurseries, the nannies were short-tempered, snapping and picking fights with one another. There was a charged feeling in the air, and the children were restless and crabby.

My morning was sounding better all the time by comparison. I was exhausted and ready to be done, but it was no more than the usual fatigue of the monthly photo day. Even so, I was more than willing to accept Dixie's offer of a cheeseburger and fries for lunch. The stress of the morning had driven her to break her New Year's diet, and she invited us to join her in the special meal. It was a rare treat to eat something other than the typical rice and beans for lunch, and in this case it meant a very filling, very fortuitous meal.

After lunch, I returned to the third floor balcony to finish the pictures I had been unable to take that morning. I took the pictures I could, then waited for the remaining few children to wake from their naps, photographing them when they did so. Finally, I was down to the last pair, a brother and sister who had become a bit of a challenge for me to photograph in recent months.

Steevenson was brought to GLA at two months old in the summer of 2008, not long after I arrived to begin my work at the orphanage.

We had watched Steevenson grow from a tiny baby to a little boy, and his happy disposition and consistently easy smiles made him one of my favorite children to photograph, not to mention a joy to spend time with. I could always count on him to take great pictures that I was proud to send to his family. Things began to change, however, when Steevenson had been with us for a little over a year. His biological parents came to visit, as they sometimes did, but this time they brought his newborn sister, whom they also wanted to give up for adoption. The staff at GLA were excited when Steevenson's adoptive parents eagerly agreed to adopt Roselaure as well; Steevenson was less thrilled. He was too young to understand their relationship in an orphanage full of children, and he had no particular interest in getting acquainted with this new baby. Steevenson especially didn't like sharing his photo-taking spotlight. The once smiling boy began to sulk and pout when he had to sit on the table with her, and after a few months he began to be challenging even when he was alone. Steevenson knew that soon Roselaure would be placed next to him, and he didn't like sharing the attention he had always enjoyed. That month, in an attempt to outwit the small boy, I was trying a new tactic that involved taking Steevenson's picture, and only Steevenson's, on the first day, so he had the attention all to himself. The next day I would bring him back to share the spotlight and take his picture together with Roselaure. Their naps had not coordinated on that Tuesday, however, so it was late afternoon by the time they were both awake and I was able to get their picture together. I will never know if that plan would eventually have succeeded, but on that particular day, it was only after being bribed with cereal that Steevenson would tolerate getting his picture taken with Roselaure.

I finished taking those last pictures around 3:30 p.m. Once I was done, it didn't take long to tear down and put away the set for that month's photos. I returned downstairs to the office, but there was little I could accomplish there. My computer had been acting up for months, and my co-worker's unfortunate computer crash over the weekend had provided the impetus I needed to run a backup on my own system. The backup had been started after work the evening before, but my computer was not known for ever doing anything quickly, and that day was no exception. By late afternoon, the estimate was saying it would still be several more hours before the backup was done. I wanted to get all the children's pictures I had taken that day off the digital camera's memory card and onto the computer, but I knew that would have to wait.

With the photos taken and my computer's files inaccessible, my options were limited. I could answer emails, surf the Internet, and watch the numbers on my computer screen tell me what percentage of the backup was complete and how many more hours until it was finished. I commiserated with the others in the office about what a long day this had been and how we could not wait for five o'clock and the end of the workday. Other than the obvious computer issues, no one in the office was able to give me details about what had gone wrong. It just seemed to have been a day when nothing had gone as planned. I, on the other hand, knew exactly why I was ready for the workday to be over. I wanted to eat dinner, take a shower, and spend the evening relaxing in my room. I kept one eye on the clock, each minute bringing me closer to quitting time. Or so I thought. In actuality, it was only one minute closer to the nightmare that was to come.

At 4:53 p.m., our lives were turned upside down. We knew that Haiti occasionally experienced earthquakes; many of us had experienced small earthquakes in Haiti before. We knew that Port-au-Prince was located on a fault line. We had even heard the geologists' predictions and warnings that it was only a matter of time, and probably not a lot of time, before Haiti experienced a major earthquake. We knew all this, but it was the kind of factual knowledge that you accept in theory yet never allow to penetrate into your day-to-day existence or plans. We were not prepared for what actually happened that day.

Suddenly, the ground was shaking—terribly, violently shaking. A thunderous roar approached ever closer, building in strength until it seemed we would be overwhelmed. It was not in the sky surrounding us. Whatever was happening was coming from the very depths of the earth that were lurching beneath us. There was confusion in the fully-charged air around us. It didn't seem possible, yet the shaking continued to grow stronger and stronger. The world was in chaos. Nothing was where it should be. Not the floors, the walls, the cabinets, or anything else. We didn't speak. We were too shocked to speak. We were busy reacting, but our world was far from silent. The windows rattled and glass shattered. Upstairs, the nannies were screaming and the babies were crying.

Panic and terror seized us in those first instants of sudden uncertainty. As best we could, we each struggled to process what was happening around us. Some of us stood frozen in shock, others frantically grasped for something to do; still others fell to their knees in prayer.

There are no words to adequately convey the experience of a major earthquake. The fear and chaos are truly indescribable. Mere words feel impersonal and sterile, yet the experience was anything but impersonal and sterile. More than anything else, the earthquake was real. In those few moments it was all-encompassing; it was the only thing we knew. There was no existence outside of the earthquake. It was our only reality. It came without regard for us or our activities, and we were powerless to do anything about it.

No one seems to know exactly how long it lasted, but thirty-five to forty seconds is the usual estimate. This is about the length of time you wait at a red light, or through an entire light cycle at a smaller intersection. It is twice as long as you are supposed to wash your hands. It is about how long it takes for a high school athlete to run 300 meters, and just under the world record for the 400-meter dash. It is the length of time it takes to say the Our Father, also called the Lord's Prayer, through twice. It is about how long it will take you to read the next paragraph. That is how long it took for everything in our world to change.

When the ground first began to shake, I was sitting at my desk in the office I shared with two co-workers. Unable to do any actual work on my computer, I was trying to organize my desk space and chatting online with a new staff member who was scheduled to arrive in Haiti in a few weeks. Leaning with my arms on the desk, I first felt the vibrations through its surface and, not immediately understanding what was happening, I pushed back, trying to get away from the strange sensation. My chair rolled easily on the tile floor and that quick movement, in addition to the earth's rocking, set me terribly off balance. I frantically looked at the floor for somewhere to focus, for a point of stability. Horrified, I realized that the floor was moving up and down in front of me like a giant seesaw. Panic rose in my chest. By now I had figured out we were experiencing an earthquake, and I looked around to see what I should do. The tall file cabinets behind me were swaying back and forth, and I was afraid they would fall and crush me. My heart was racing, and in three quick steps I ran the ten feet to the entrance of Dixie's office, where I sought shelter in the doorframe.

Dixie also tried to find refuge in the doorway. Her husband, John, stayed in his office behind hers, but at the earth's first movement he had quickly understood what was happening and yelled for everyone to move to the shelter of a doorway. Dixie attempted to rise from her chair, only to twice be thrown back into it. Finally she succeeded in standing, but the battle was not yet over. Walking was no easy task, and her desk was a large obstacle in the way. She used the desk to her advantage, however, holding on to it for support as she made her way to the door. We leaned against opposite doorposts and looked at each other and the chaos going on around us with wide, disbelieving eyes. Time dragged, each second an eternal lifetime.

Back in the main office, Laurie and Stephanie were stuck in their seats, holding onto whatever was at hand while the storm raged around them. They say that animals sense danger before humans, and Bruno, a six-month-old Great Dane, certainly became agitated in the moments before the shaking began. He was pestering Laurie, who had turned around to try to calm him when the ground shuddered and the heavy wooden cabinet behind her began to fall. Laurie put her arms out to stop it from crushing her, but she was unable to move from her chair, pinned beneath the cabinet's weight.

The walls continued shaking, and the floor tossed about like waves on the sea. Nothing was as it should be. Nothing was still. Perhaps even we were shaking in terror, but it was impossible to tell, with how violently the earth was moving beneath us. Not even a minute earlier, we had been engrossed in our normal activities, oblivious to our imminent danger. Now we were experiencing what could only be classified as a major earthquake. It seemed that it would never stop, and it lasted more than long enough for us to wonder if it ever would.

At last the shaking stilled, and we faced the nightmare that had now become our reality.

CHAPTER 2

THE FIRST NIGHT

In this world you will have trouble.
But take heart! I have overcome the world.

~ John 16:33b

THE SUDDEN SILENCE WAS ALMOST as surprising as the shaking had been when it started, moments earlier. The silence lasted only about half a second, however, before John barged out of his office, ushering us outside with urgent directives and an insistent tone: "Get out! Get out!" He wanted us away from any dangerous aftereffects of the quake, and out of the way so he could inspect the building and assess its condition. Instinctively, I wanted to go upstairs to the nursery, but John spoke in a voice I didn't dare question. I didn't believe anything was wrong upstairs; I only wanted to see the children, to hold them, to *know* they were where I had left them. Instead, I obediently filed outside with the others from the office, feeling dizzy and lightheaded. At the time, I thought the earthquake had shaken us so vigorously for so long that it had thrown off my equilibrium. Maybe it did, but I hadn't yet realized the truth that the ground beneath us was still in motion and would be for weeks to come.

The volunteers and visiting families soon joined us in front of the main house. They had been upstairs on the balcony and in the nurseries when the earthquake hit, and they assured us that the children were all safe. Most of the volunteers had brought babies downstairs with them, and several of the parents had carried another child in addition to their own. I eagerly took one of those children into my arms, thankful to have someone to hold. It was a comfort to me, but more than that, the small gesture of holding a child close was the only thing I could do. My life, and that child's, had suddenly spun out of control. There was nothing I could do about that, but I could try to make him feel a little more secure.

GLA's only non-Haitian staff member upstairs at the time of the earthquake was Susan, a pediatric nurse. Susan spent her days in the four nurseries, and she was used to the busyness and chaos of the late afternoon hour. The children were awake from their naps, but many of them were still cranky and fussing. A few were crying in their cribs, while those who could climb out were wandering around the rooms. All of them were hungry, and children and nannies alike were looking forward to the dinner hour.

All day long, Susan had been feeling an uneasiness combined with a sense of inexplicable dread. Like the rest of us, she was anxious for the workday to end. She spent most of her time in the NICU nursery—named after the neo-natal intensive care unit in hospitals—and that is where she was at 4:53 p.m. on January 12. Susan was moving to pick up one of the children, a sick baby who was crying, when the rumbling started and advanced into something far deeper, far more terrible. Bruises on her arms later showed that she was thrown into the crib while she was picking up the child, but Susan felt no pain. Holding the baby to her chest, Susan fell to her knees, using her body to shield another child who had been playing on the floor nearby. She felt a deep regret that she could not protect everyone, but she was going to do everything she could for those two nearest to her. Susan heard the great rumble, felt the ground shaking, and believed that the house was collapsing. She was sure that we were all going to die when it did. Equipment and medicines crashed to the ground, and the nannies around her were crying out to God at the top of their voices. Susan stayed on her knees, still shielding the two babies, praying and waiting out the longest forty seconds any of us had ever known.

Suddenly there was silence; the house had stood. We had experienced a major earthquake, but the house was still standing. Dazed and taking deep breaths to calm herself, Susan looked around the nursery, assessing the situation. The youngest and most fragile children were in this room, and as her eyes found each of them, she quickly saw that every one of them was safe. It seemed unbelievable, especially considering the medical supplies that had been thrown from their shelves and were now cluttering the floor and some of the cribs. One crib in particular was full of debris, and Susan looked again at baby Atlanta on the floor. She was overcome with thankfulness as she remembered lifting the child out of her crib and placing her on the floor only a few minutes earlier. That simple act had very likely saved Atlanta's life.

Susan felt nauseous and had the same out-of-balance sensation that the rest of us were experiencing. At first she thought it was a physical reaction to her emotions, possibly even the beginnings of hysteria. While she was looking around, however, she noticed the IV pole swaying, and Susan recognized her disorientation for what it was—the ground was still moving, and she was experiencing motion sickness.

Susan saw that the babies in front of her were okay, but were the children in the other three nurseries as fortunate? As quickly as possible she secured the room, moving heavy items that were still on the shelves to a safer place closer to the ground and clearing away the supplies that had crashed to the floor. Once Susan was satisfied that the room was as safe as she could make it, she hurried to the other nurseries to see how the rest of the children had fared.

Susan first went to the Urgence A nursery on the opposite side of the house. The children there were ten to fifteen months old, and they were the next youngest and most fragile after the NICU babies. Powder, diaper cream, and extra clothes were strewn across the floor; the PVC pipes used as curtain rods had been shaken loose and were hanging precariously above children's heads. The stacked wooden cribs hadn't fallen over, though, and the babies in them were fine. Everyone in this nursery was safe as well.

The entrance to Urgence B and the main nursery was halfway between Urgence A and the NICU, and Susan quickly retraced her steps. She entered Urgence B, a smaller nursery with children thirteen to eighteen months old, and saw that everything was under control. The cribs in this nursery were more solid and stable, and the kids were all safe and out of the way inside of them.

Susan hurried through Urgence B and opened the half door into the main nursery. There the scene was more chaotic. The oldest children at the main house were in this nursery, most of them between the ages of eighteen and thirty months. Many of the nannies had run outside in panic when the earth first shook, and the ones who remained were frightened and hysterical. Several of the children were crying, reacting to the emotions of their caregivers. Others were sitting on the floor, silently looking around in dazed confusion, not understanding what was happening in their world. Still others were going about their normal activities: running through the nursery, climbing into cribs, and seeing what mischief they could get into with all the nannies distracted. The only injuries Susan found, however, were minor bumps and bruises. It seemed unbelievable, but not one child or adult in the house had suffered severe injury.

Greatly relieved to find that everyone was alive and well, Susan went back around and inspected each room more carefully. By this time, some of the nannies who had run outside during the earthquake were returning. Susan met one of these nannies in the hall, and they hugged one another in shared grief. They had no words of comfort to offer, only the knowledge and understanding that whatever had just happened to our world, we were all in it together. This entire time several more earthquakes—aftershocks—had been shaking us.

The only evidence of the earthquake's destruction immediately visible from GLA's main house was a neighbor's hut that had been destroyed. Piles of cement rubble were now all that remained where the house had stood only minutes before. Susan saw the damage from a nursery balcony, and it was a dark glimpse of Haiti's new reality; she realized that the earthquake had been devastating.

Those of us in the yard had not yet witnessed the earthquake's destruction, but we knew it could only be horrific. We didn't know where the earthquake had been centered, but as strongly as we had felt it, Port-au-Prince, less than ten miles away, must also have experienced it. The capital city was overcrowded, filled with masses of impoverished Haitians who lived in poorly constructed shacks, many of which had been destroyed. No one had to tell us this; we knew it was true. There was no other possible outcome. We had no idea of the extent of the damage, and our best guesses didn't even come close to the actual scope, but we knew immediately that it must be bad—very, very bad. We held the children close in our arms and tried to comfort them and one another. We looked up to the windows of the nurseries and saw the familiar faces of precious children smiling down on us. In that moment all we knew was that our house was standing and that no one in it was hurt.

Phone service was difficult, but that didn't stop Laurie and me from trying to call others in Haiti to learn their situation. After several attempts, I was relieved to get through to a staff member at the toddler house. She assured me that no one there had been injured and that their buildings had stood, as well; everything was fine and under control. I could picture the scene that had played out so recently at the toddler house . . .

It was late afternoon, almost dinnertime, and the scent of garlic permeated the air as the kitchen staff finished cooking the evening meal. Naps were over and school was out for the day, so the children were all outside in the courtyard with the nannies. They were waiting to be called to dinner and were happily engaged in their normal activities. A group of older girls stood giggling in a cluster by the playset deck, busily comparing the stickers they had recently added to their notebooks. Another older child, a boy, sat off by himself, diligently studying the schoolwork he had been given and working to finish it as quickly as possible. The younger kids had no thought of homework and were busy in their various groups and activities. A few children were playing on the swings, pumping their legs harder and harder to go as high as they possibly could. Two lucky boys were riding around on the prized scooters, racing back and forth across the yard. The youngest children of all were content to sit near their nannies and observe the scene around them. There was always plenty to watch in the antics of the older children.

Without warning, the trembling began, bringing with it a momentary confusion. The children looked to their nannies, many running to them for comfort. A few were knocked to the ground by the violence of the shaking. Several children who had been inside—using the bathroom, retrieving something from their rooms, or running errands—quickly ran outside. Nannies and older children grabbed the hands of the younger ones and pulled them out into the yard, away from the swaying buildings. Soon everyone was outside, staring in disbelief at the convulsing structures and at the parked car that bounced as if it were alive.

When the earth stilled, the nannies looked at each other in amazement over the heads of the children. Those who first recovered from the shock directed the children to sit down in an open area. The scene was remarkably similar to the one playing out half a mile down the road, where we waited outside at GLA's main house.

Adults were seeking to comfort the children and give them a sense of certainty and security that they themselves didn't feel. When the earthquake began, many of the nannies at both houses had believed the world was ending. Maybe that belief was not so far off the mark; Haiti would certainly never be the same. The nannies feared for their families, their loved ones, their homes, and for their country. From the toddler house yard, there was a mountain that blocked the view of Port-au-Prince, but a giant cloud of dust could be seen rising from the city, a disheartening sign of the damage that had been caused by the violent earthquake.

When I called, everyone at the toddler house was waiting outside while they determined what to do next. They were close enough to the guesthouse to see that it was still standing, as well. It was a huge relief to know that not only were we okay at our house, but that the other children and staff had survived the earthquake as well. Even though there were still many uncertainties and questions regarding others we knew—people we were not able to get in touch with—all of GLA was intact. After that quick phone call, I would not be able to make another for nearly a week. Phone service in Haiti was down or otherwise jammed.

While we waited outside at the main house, John inspected the building for damage. The house was still standing, but he checked to make sure that the structure was still strong and that there were no breaks in the water or gas lines. Although John found some cracks in the exterior molding, there were none in the structure itself. He marked the ends of the cracks so he could continue to monitor them for growth in the coming days. After nearly forty minutes outside, John gave the all clear for us to return to the house.

The scene that met us when we reentered the house was a brutal reminder of the earthquake we had just experienced, as well as a glimpse into the fate of a nation. Everything was in disarray. The common room floor was littered with books, pictures, and broken knick-knacks that had crashed to the floor. Somehow, the ground's shaking had unlatched the china cabinet: glasses and bowls lay shattered on the tile floor beneath it. In the kitchen, serving bowls, dishes, and spoons were now on the floor. The kitchen staff had been in the process of dishing up the children's food at the time of the earthquake, and many of those bowls were now upside down on the floor, with corn mush and bean sauce spilled out around them. One bowl somehow landed right side up, the food in it ready to be served. Our tightly packed storage depots, both upstairs and down, were now strewn with various canned goods, boxes of food, cartons of formula, and bottles of soap and hand sanitizer. Shelves had broken in the supply depot, and in the food depot two boxes of brownies had fallen onto six flats of eggs that, amazingly, were still intact. Our office desks were disorganized and cluttered. Computer monitors, framed photos, files, toys, and nearly everything else that had been sitting on our desks had toppled, and supplies from the surrounding cabinets had spilled onto them as well.

The house was truly a disordered mess, but in that moment it didn't matter. We had suddenly reverted to the most basic of needs. None of the material possessions that had been damaged were worth comparing to the lives that had been spared. We were alive. Those around us were alive, and that was what mattered. For the time being, it was enough.

The Haitian staff retrieved mops and brooms, and the volunteers helped with the cleanup. They threw away the broken pieces, swept up the shards of glass, and replaced the undamaged items on their shelves or on a table closer to ground level.

In addition to assessing the situation, our first priority was to let our families, friends, and supporters back home know that we were well. It was forty minutes after the earthquake when we returned to the office, and already I had received emails and several instant messages from people at home wanting to know if I was safe. Had I survived? Was I in any immediate danger? Everyone else had received similar messages from home, and Laurie and I encouraged Dixie to post an update on the GLA website. We all knew that when the adoptive families and GLA supporters heard about the earthquake, they would check the site for news about their children's safety and our current situation. Each of us also posted messages on our personal Facebook pages, and the responses we received were overwhelming. News about Haiti's earthquake was already circling the globe, and that gave us another window into the scope of the disaster. It was around this time, once we were back inside and able to get online, that we learned the magnitude of that first earthquake: 7.0. It was stronger than I had realized, and it was one more reason to fear the damage it had caused and the aftermath we would soon be forced to deal with.

As we sat at our desks, the aftershocks continued. Over and over, the ground would lurch and rock beneath us. When the trembling started, we didn't know how strong it would become or how long it would last. The fight-or-flight instinct was strong. Every time I felt a jolt, I would jump up and run back to the doorway, my "safe" place. Usually it didn't last long enough for me to even reach the door, but it always left my heart pounding and my breathing rapid. As soon as my body would finally relax and my panic would subside, another tremor would shake us. Between the aftershocks there was a constant rolling, as if we were on a big ship in a stormy sea. After several large aftershocks within only a few minutes, Dixie decided that was enough: everyone had to go back outside. This was actually a relief, as our rattled nerves could not take much more of the constant strain, and we didn't seem to feel the movement quite as strongly out in the open.

Staff and volunteers helped take all the children and necessary supplies to the open area in front of the house. We gathered blankets from everywhere we could find them, laying them out for the children to sit and lie on. Collecting blankets from storage in the upstairs bathroom, I perched precariously on the diaper-changing table to reach them. The plastic tubs of supplies were stacked on shelves, and the blankets were at the very top. Although I was terrified that an aftershock would knock me to the floor, I was grateful to have some concrete way to help. I was even more grateful once I had retrieved the blankets and climbed back down to the relative safety of the ground. At that point, there was nowhere near Port-au-Prince that could truly be called "stable," but the floor was certainly the better option.

By this time it was dark outside. Although it was only about an hour after the sun had set, nights in Haiti are much darker than in more developed countries. The sun disappears quickly so close to the equator, and there is minimal artificial light, even in the cities. By 6:30 p.m. the sky was pitch black; it might as well have been the middle of the night. Our generator-powered security lights did little to illuminate the yard, but at least we had that small amount of light. The shadowy darkness only heightened the sense that our familiar world had suddenly become unfamiliar and foreign.

The kitchen ladies brought the big pots of food outside and began filling bowls for the children. We knew there was going to be no such thing as normal or routine for that night, and the children needed to be fed as soon as possible. It was already over an hour past their dinnertime, and they didn't know what was going on around them or why they were outside at night. They were hungry and confused. Everyone pitched in to feed the kids, and we did our best to assure them that everything was going to be all right—even though we were afraid it never would be again.

I numbly retrieved a bowl of food and searched for Kerderns, my little buddy, who was just a few months away from his third birthday. He was toward the outside of the cluster of kids, near where I had seen him not long before. Several times in the past hours, I had felt the need to be near him and to spend a few moments sharing a hug that was as comforting to me as it was to him. Kerderns had been at the orphanage since before I arrived, and we had quickly become special friends. As I fed him his *mayi* (corn mush) with bean sauce, Kerderns smiled at me with trust in his eyes. I held him close, but a part of me wanted to run far away from the responsibility of caring for not only him, but also the nearly one hundred other children spread out on the blankets around me. The present circumstances were out of my control—the past hours had proven that beyond a doubt. I would do everything I could to care for Kerderns and the others, but I knew it might not be enough. I could not promise them tomorrow. That simple truth terrified me and broke my heart.

All this time, frequent aftershocks rocked us. From the time of the first quake earlier in the evening, the earth had never stopped shaking. Even when we thought we were still, we were not. If we looked up at the trees or the basketball hoop, we could see that the motion of the earth was causing them to sway. When we were sitting on the ground, we could feel the vibrations through every part of us; they never stopped. In spite of everything happening around them, though, the children adjusted well to their circumstances. The babies were falling asleep, and many of the other children were showing signs of drowsiness as well. Some of the more energetic children were running around in the open spaces. They didn't understand why we were all outside, but while they had this unexpected freedom, they intended to make the most of it. Occasionally we had to direct them to safe areas, but generally we left them to their games.

By now the adults' dinner had also been brought outside, and once the children had been fed, we began to eat as well. I doubt that many of us had an appetite that night, but we knew that what we had already experienced was only the beginning of what was to come. We knew that we would need our strength for the days ahead not only for ourselves, but also to care for the children. So we ate. Once I convinced myself that my body would tolerate food, I dished out a few small spoonfuls, enough to pass as an appropriate serving, and found a place near the edge of the blankets. While I was eating my macaroni casserole, the older children came running up to me and I shared my food with them. Several of them took a bite, but only Rénalia kept coming back for more. I think she might have eaten more than I did, but that was fine with me: I wasn't hungry, anyway.

The scene around me was surreal, as if I was watching someone else's life, not living my own. I realized that the hard cement beneath me was not as solid as I had always believed it to be, nor was my life as stable as I like to think. The blanket-strewn yard around me was proof of that. Nannies huddled together on short walls and in the back of pickup trucks, offering each other whatever comfort they could. Many of them had cell phones to their ears, trying unsuccessfully to reach loved ones at home. I had loaned my phone to one of the nannies, and every time I asked if she had been able to get through to her family, she shook her head with haunted, grief-filled eyes. She kept trying, but was never able to reach them that night.

Susan was monitoring all of the children for signs of sickness, spending the majority of her time with those who were the most fragile or were already battling illness: Darline had a heart condition, Atlanta was our newest baby and was severely malnourished, and there were several other children who were also under Susan's watchful eye that night. The volunteers were scattered among the children, the strain evident on their frightened faces. I suspect mine looked the same. The adoptive parents visiting that week held their children close to them, as if they could keep them safe through the sheer force of their will.

There were many questions running through our heads that night: uncertainties about the future, concern for our present situation, worry for loved ones throughout Haiti, and even confusion as to how we came to be in this situation. We were in the middle of a huge natural disaster with no warning, no preparation, and certainly no going back. In spite of the thin veil of hope that this was all some-how a bad dream, we were all acutely aware that this disaster was our new reality.

As the children settled down for the night, the staff and visitors started going inside, a few at a time, to check the news on TV or the Internet. Our television had satellite service, which had not been damaged and would now be permanently fixed on CNN for the in-definite future. Others wanted to connect with family and friends online, and they read the Haitian earthquake articles, whose news headlines were quickly filling cyberspace. Even though we had expe-rienced the earthquake, the news we were receiving seemed incom-prehensible. As the night continued, we heard more and more stories of loss. It was a long and unbelievable list: the presidential palace, the national cathedral, the port, the Caribbean Supermarket, the Hotel Montana, and on and on. These were national landmarks and presti-gious places in Haiti. These were places that seemed as much a part of the nation as the mountains and the sea. These places were a part of our lives and our routine. These were the types of places one ex-pects to be solid and strong: places that do not just go away. Yet, sud-denly—they were gone. And if these enduring landmarks had fallen, was *anything* in Port-au-Prince left standing?

Throughout the night, people gathered around the TV in the liv-ing room, trying to learn what they could about what was happening just a few miles down the road. I walked through that room many times, catching snatches of news reports as I passed from the office to outside and back again. At one point I stopped for a few minutes, together with several other staff members. The news showed a scene from Florida: reporters interviewing passengers who had been on the runway in Port-au-Prince during the earthquake. The plane had taken off immediately afterwards and arrived in Miami a couple of hours later. The passengers being interviewed were still visibly shaken by what had happened. I understood their emotions, and my eyes stung with unshed tears. Instinctively, I knew that if I cried, I would not be able to stop, and I had no time for tears. Instead of crying, I left the room, went back to work, and didn't watch the news again.

In the office, Dixie and I worked at our desks, communicating with the outside world via the Internet and satellite telephone. Dixie was working with GLA's US office in Colorado and with board members to spread the word that we were safe, and to plan the response for the coming days. I was doing my best to respond to the adoptive parents' inquiries about GLA and their children's health and safety. I also kept busy emailing photos. Laurie had gone around the house shortly after the earthquake and taken pictures of the chaos it had caused. In the following hours, I took pictures of the scene outside, where the children and adults were sitting in the dimly lit yard, waiting for the shaking to stop. I then sent these photos to the Colorado office to help them understand our current situation and for them to post online.

That first night I didn't sit at my desk; instead, I pushed the chair in and stood behind it. The earth's motion was too intense and I felt it too strongly when I sat down. More significantly, however, the aftershocks were continuing, and I wanted to be able to react as quickly as possible, not be stuck in a chair.

Outside, the children were still on the blanket-covered ground, a few nannies lying down in the middle of them. Most of the children slept, but a few sat quietly, looking around wide-eyed, as if still trying to figure out what had become of their world. The nannies prayed aloud and sang many different hymns and songs to God. The one they sang most often was "How Great Thou Art." Their voices rose above the hushed atmosphere, filling the emptiness and bringing hope and a sense of peace amid the confusion. A short distance away at the toddler house, the same song rang out as the ladies there led the children in singing as well. Our nannies at both houses struggled with uncertainty, unable to communicate with their families. The pain and tension on their faces was nearly tangible, as they tried over and over to call their loved ones. Had their children survived? What had happened to their mothers, fathers, brothers, sisters, husbands, boyfriends, and neighbors? Did they still have a house? What was left of their world? Had they lost everyone and everything they loved? They didn't yet know the answers to these questions; what they did know was that their God was sovereign, and they trusted that they could depend on Him, whatever the circumstances turned out to be.

After we had been outside for several hours, the Bickels' fourteen-year-old son Mark finally arrived home. He had been at his school near Petionville when the earthquake hit. At one point Mark had managed to contact his family by phone, so they knew that he was safe. Still, it was a tremendous relief to see him actually walk through the gate, alive and well and home at last. Mark wasn't injured, but he and the teacher who had brought him home told a grim story of what they had seen. Along the road they had travelled, nearly every other building had collapsed, and they had driven around dead bodies lying in the streets. And their route had been through one of the better parts of the city. We all knew that it would be much worse in the heart of Port-au-Prince, where the poorest people lived.

This news was just one more report of the tragedy that was continuing to unfold. None of us had been optimistic in our outlook to begin with, but each new accounting only further confirmed what we were afraid to be true. The only good news we received with Mark's arrival was that we now knew the roads were clear. It would be possible for us to get supplies . . . if there were any supplies available.

Around ten o'clock that night, Dixie instructed everyone to take the children back inside the house. The aftershocks seemed to be weakening, and the children would be warmer and more comfortable in their own beds. The parade of children marched inside and up the stairs, adults spread throughout the route to guide them to their nurseries. We carried the younger children and made sure everyone was settled into their beds. Once the children were where they belonged and well on the way to falling back to sleep, the adults returned to the yard to clean the littered area. We gathered blankets, separating out the clean ones to be used again, and collected the dirty bowls, spoons, bottles, and cups that had been used for the evening meal, as well as any food that was still lying around. We threw out the trash and the many dirty diapers we found.

While we were cleaning up, one of the Haitian staff members, Vivianne, questioned me about the earthquake—about what had happened and what was to come. I was as new to earthquakes as she was, but I did have the advantage of education and previous media exposure to them.

"What's going to happen next?" Vivianne asked me, fear etched onto her face.

I told her that I honestly didn't know. I knew that the earth would continue to shake, but I had no idea how long. Vivianne understood that the earth's plates had moved and caused the shaking, since Susan had already explained about aftershocks and that the earth was trying to settle back into a comfortable place.

"How long will the aftershocks last?"

Again, I didn't know the answer, nor was anything I did know something either of us wanted to hear. I had already learned that the experts were talking about weeks of aftershocks, possibly lasting into months. It was something none of us wanted to think about, least of all that night.

Vivianne's last question was the hardest: "Will there be another earthquake as big as the first one?"

It was the question that was haunting all of us in the recesses of our minds. Vivianne wanted reassurance that we would not have another, bigger earthquake. I wanted the same reassurance, but no such promise could be given. All I could tell her—and myself—was that aftershocks usually get smaller instead of bigger. It seemed unlikely that we would have to live through another earthquake as bad as 7.0, but there were no guarantees.

What was nearly certain was that there would be more aftershocks. They would shake the house again. There was no comfort in those words for either of us, but they were the truth. Comforting lies would only provide a shallow reassurance, one that would cause more pain when it was ripped away innumerable times in the days ahead.

Vivianne and I solemnly finished clearing the yard, and then we went our separate ways.

At last, we could begin to think about putting the terrible day behind us. We could turn our attention toward getting some rest, before the difficult days we knew were to come. After wearily checking to confirm that there was nothing more to do, no more responsibilities that would not wait until the next day, we started returning to our rooms. It was around 11:00 p.m. when I first entered my room, more than six hours after the initial earthquake. Susan, my roommate, had told me that things were displaced but generally undamaged. However, since the main house had been straightened and put back in order hours earlier, it was a shock for me to see my room for the first time: things were still knocked over, moved around, and had fallen off shelves. Bathroom toiletries were scattered on the floor and in the sink. Powder had spilled everywhere. Surprisingly, nothing breakable had fallen, our laptops were unharmed, and even our drinking water had not spilled out of our glasses! At that moment, I don't believe I would have cared if everything had been destroyed, but I was certainly thankful it was not.

Susan and I straightened our room enough to make it livable and less cluttered. Many of the things that had fallen we set aside on the floor or the lower shelves, and other items we placed lower to the ground. We didn't want anything else falling, especially things that might injure us or were likely to break. This was the first quiet time we had since before the earthquake changed everything. We finally had time to sit and think—although we didn't want to think too much—about what had happened and what was going to happen next. We had time to talk through some of the things we had experienced, and time to send out personal emails assuring family and friends back home that we truly were all right.

During the course of the evening, I don't think a ten-minute period passed without at least one aftershock. Not long after the kids had returned inside, we experienced several more strong aftershocks of 5.5 or higher. Unwilling to spend the night in the shaking building, the nannies moved all the children back outside shortly after midnight. They got out the blankets we had so recently put away and did their best to shelter themselves and the children from the cold night air.

Susan was concerned about several of the more fragile children sleeping outside, so she brought four of them into our room. We placed mattresses on our floor and laid the children on them. Darline and Lovely were worn out from the long day and the unusual events of the evening, and the two of them quickly settled down. Jean Luc was older, a few months past his second birthday, and uncertain about exactly what was happening around him. He had been at the orphanage for some time, however, and he had an implicit trust in Susan. If she was near, his world was all right. It was baby Atlanta who had the most trouble that night. She was our newest child, having arrived only the week before. Atlanta wanted to be held and loved, to feel secure. There had been so many changes in her life recently. We did what we could to reassure her, but we couldn't hold her all night, as she wanted. Finally we gave her a small plush animal to hold and that seemed to comfort her, at least enough that she fell asleep.

In spite of our exhaustion, it was difficult for many of the adults to sleep. The constant shaking and rocking of the earth could be felt when standing, more when sitting, and most of all when lying down. The whole bed seemed to sway beneath me. It was a feeling we would soon come to know and accept as "normal," but that first night it was still foreign and highly disconcerting. For some of the staff, sleep was a blessed relief from the stress and chaos of the preceding hours. For others, it was a frightening chasm of nightmares and fears that overactive minds would not allow.

That night was a time of uncertainty and confusion. We didn't know what was to come, and we had not yet had enough experience with earthquakes to truly know how bad it would prove to be. We only knew it was catastrophic. It had to be. Our very foundation had shaken, and our house was solidly built. Much of the population of Haiti, though, lived in dilapidated shacks, some no more than sticks tied together and leaned against another building. They barely provided shelter from the elements, and they were certainly no match for the constantly shaking ground. Nothing was built to withstand that, and the world was about to learn just how ill-prepared Haiti was to survive a major earthquake.

CHAPTER 3

INTERNATIONAL NEWS

No man is an island, entire of itself;
Every man is a piece of the continent, a part of the main.
~ John Donne, Meditation XVII

AS EARTH SHATTERING AS OUR experience had been, the rest of the world went on with life as usual, oblivious to the plight of millions, at least at first. It didn't take long, however, for news of the earthquake to reach the rest of the world. Within fifteen minutes of the initial quake, major news outlets were announcing that there had been an earthquake in Haiti.

One of the first to learn the news was Tom, a GLA board member, who was working at his computer a little after 5:00 p.m., when he saw a tweet from the Los Angeles Times reporting an earthquake in Haiti. He immediately got on instant messenger with Jean in GLA's Colorado office to see what she knew. Since Jean was also talking with John in Haiti at the same time, she had the authoritative news that GLA, its buildings, and everyone on the premises were all okay. Assured of everyone's safety, Tom was able to move past his initial concern and on to the next logical step in his mind: *what can I do now to help from here?* He remained at his computer, but his entire focus and purpose had changed.

Once Jean finished her conversation with John, she had phone calls of her own to make. One of those calls was to John and Dixie's son Patrick and his wife Holli, who worked in the US office with Jean. Holli had taken a day off from work to help Patrick paint their house. They were getting it ready to rent so they could move to Haiti to work at GLA there. Patrick answered his cell phone, and Jean told him the news. Having spent many of his growing-up years in Haiti, Patrick had experienced several minor earthquakes, and at first he and Holli went back to painting the house, assuming this was simply another one like those. Unable to shake the thoughts of the earthquake, however, he and Holli went to a neighbor's house to try to get more information. As soon as they turned on CNN, they saw Wolf Blitzer talking about Haiti's earthquake, with estimates coming in for either a magnitude 7.5 or 7.2. A map showed the epicenter in Carrefour, uncomfortably close to the mountains where GLA—and their family—was located. Patrick and Holli kept watching the news, but the reporters had little new information to share, and kept repeating what they did know over and over.

In Iowa, Jaime, one of our adoptive parents, was going through a fast food drive-through on the way to piano lessons when she got a call on her cell phone. It was her mother: "What do you know about Haiti?" Jaime was confused by the question and uncertain how to answer. Jaime and her husband were in the process of adopting six-year-old twins from GLA, so obviously Haiti was often on their hearts and minds. When Jaime's mother realized that Jaime didn't understand what she was asking, she explained, "There was a huge earthquake in Haiti. I wondered if you know if the kids are okay."

Jaime immediately began to tremble and became very cold. She got off the phone with her mother and called her husband, Jason. He hadn't yet heard anything, either, but he called Tom, who was able to reassure them that everyone at GLA was all right.

Jason and Jaime were relieved and overjoyed to know that the twins were safe. As the night wore on, however, they began to worry about how this would affect their adoption and the process of bringing their children home. Jean Dany and Danise's adoption was legally complete, and Jason and Jaime had hoped to have all the necessary passports and visas by the upcoming summer. Where was their adoption paperwork now? Had the legal documents survived, or were they now buried in the rubble somewhere in Port-au-Prince? Once the questions started, they kept coming: How were the kids doing emotionally? Were they scared of the aftershocks—and how long were the aftershocks going to last? Would the buildings at GLA continue to stand up to the nearly constant shaking?

They tried to get as much information as they could about the earthquake and the overall conditions in Haiti. They also updated family and friends on the situation and let everyone know that their kids were safe. Then Jason and Jaime and their two daughters at home prayed together for Jean Dany and Danise, GLA, and the nation of Haiti.

My own parents, at home in Indiana, received a similar phone call. A friend from church called to see if my parents knew about the earthquake or had any news from me. Since I was still outside at the time, they didn't, and they immediately switched the TV to a news station and got online. They had both visited Haiti previously and knew enough to understand what such a disaster would mean for the nation. After about twenty minutes of uncertainty, I came online and was able to assure them that I was safe. They were still concerned, especially about the ongoing situation and our ability to get supplies, but they were relieved to hear from me and to know that I had survived.

GLA's newest staff member, Melissa, was at home in Manitoba, and she was also waiting on me to get back online. We had been chatting on instant messenger, but at the first shaking, all thoughts of that conversation had fled my mind. Having left Haiti only three weeks earlier, Melissa was familiar with how our office ran, and she assumed I had been called away to some task or another. She had also been chatting with another friend in Haiti, who suddenly disappeared at the same time I did. Her other friend got back online first, talking about dishes falling onto the floor and other things Melissa didn't understand, until she said that there had been an earthquake. At that point Melissa became eager to hear news from anyone at GLA. She took hope in the fact that our house was only a few miles away from her friend's, which she knew was still standing. Within a few more minutes I returned to the office and the forgotten conversation. Melissa was greatly relieved to hear that everybody was okay. She had already been busy making plans to get back to Haiti, and she was now more determined than ever to get there as quickly as possible.

On the other side of the world, Alain and Fernanda were watching the late night news in Luxembourg when they saw that there had been an earthquake in Haiti. Their first thoughts were for their children, Ronalson and Fabien, who were so far away. Had they survived? They continued to watch TV to learn as much as they could about what was happening in Haiti, but the news they most wanted to hear was not likely to be on the television. They had no contact with anyone from GLA, and it was not until Thursday that they finally knew for sure that their children were alive, healthy, and unharmed. It had been an anxious couple of days, watching the news coverage and hoping for the best but fearing the worst. At last they knew, and they wholeheartedly thanked God for protecting their sons.

While the time difference meant that the European families were nearing the end of the day when news of the earthquake began to reach the world, on the western coast of the United States it was still early afternoon. In Oregon, Jill received an email half an hour after the earthquake from a friend, another adoptive mother, who had heard the terrible news. Jill started searching the Internet for more information, and what she found was disheartening. As she and her friend continued emailing, sharing their fears and confusion with one another, the news came that everyone at GLA was alive and well. This was obviously a huge relief for them, but it didn't take away the confusion and the worry for their sons, their adoptions, and the people at GLA whom they had learned to call friends.

Jill and her husband, Joe, had just spent two wonderful weeks at GLA with Chancelet over Christmas, and they struggled to comprehend that the Haiti they had so recently visited was facing this tragedy. Their hearts were broken, for Chancelet of course, but also for the Haitian people whom they had come to know and love.

Joe and Jill knew only one way to overcome their anxiety and concern, and that was to do whatever they could to help. Joe took a leave of absence from work and told Dixie that if she needed his help in any way, all she had to do was let him know and he would be on a plane to Haiti. Jill started many email and phone conversations with family and friends. She was trying to make sense of everything that was happening, but also trying to find her role in all of this. She began talking with Tom and realized that with her communications and marketing background, she could help lead the campaign to raise awareness and funds to help GLA and Haiti.

About fifty miles south, another GLA family was also learning the terrible news. A friend called Anita to ask if she had heard about the earthquake in Haiti. Anita had not, but she quickly got off the phone so she could look for details on the Internet. Rather than the expected adrenaline rush or even concern for her children in Haiti, Anita felt numb with the shock of the news. It didn't take her long to find updates on Facebook, assuring her that all the children and staff were safe. With the comfort of that knowledge, Anita went to CNN's website and saw the first hint of how bad the earthquake really was, and what a blessing it was that Rémy and Erlande and everyone else at GLA had survived.

Anita and her husband Russ talked on the phone, sharing their information and their grief. Their children were alive, but Haiti was in ruins. Tens of thousands of people had died, and the situation seemed hopeless and frightening. Russ and Anita took comfort in one another and especially in who their God was. In spite of how their circumstances had suddenly spun out of control, they knew that their lives, and the lives of their children, were not out of God's control.

Anita spent the rest of the afternoon praying and watching TV for news. When her daughters returned home from school, she was thankful that she already had news about their Haitian brother and sister, especially since her oldest daughter had learned about the earthquake before she arrived home. Anita was able to reassure them that Rémy and Erlande were alive and well, but she wished that she could as easily assure herself and Russ that everything was going to be okay. This crisis had the potential to add innumerable months or even years to their adoption. They had hoped their children would be joining the family within the next six months, and they saw that possibility buried in the rubble they saw on their television screen. Throughout the evening, friends and family called, and each time Russ or Anita would answer people's questions with an "I don't know," it seemed that much truer that the kids would be staying in their devastated homeland for the foreseeable future.

As a mother, Anita wanted to be with her children. She hated the fact that they had experienced such a tragedy, especially since she was not there to hold and comfort them through it. Twice she got up from bed to dress and go to the airport to fly to Haiti. She realized how fruitless this would be, though, so she stopped herself from even going out the door. Anita recognized that it wasn't enough to say that she trusted God. She was going to have to live that trust, and she knew it would not be easy.

Within an hour of the quake, two women on different continents opened the same email. It was an email with the subject heading "Earthquake in Haiti" sent to members of a Yahoo! group for GLA adoptive families.

In Chicago, Samantha was preparing to print some pictures for an album she was putting together for her son. When she saw the email, her heart stopped, and she hurried to open the email. The message was short, stating that everyone at GLA was okay. With that immediate concern answered, Samantha began scouring the Internet for more information, searching the websites of major news organizations, GLA, and anyone else she could think of that might give her some insight into the situation. Having previously lived through several large quakes in California, Samantha had a better understanding of earthquakes than most of the adoptive parents. She wanted to know exactly what "okay" meant to GLA, how strong the earthquake had been, and where the epicenter was in proximity to the orphanage. She was also concerned about the mental state of the children and staff at GLA.

Samantha continued to watch the news, both online and on television, hoping to find answers to as many of her questions as possible. Little information was available at that point, though, and they kept repeating the same pictures and few known facts over and over. Samantha was anxious for any new information; she especially wanted to see the effects of the aftershocks she knew Haiti would be experiencing. She also spoke with family and friends, sharing whatever she had learned with them.

Mostly, though, Samantha worried about her adoptive son, Widkelly, and how he was coping with the physical and emotional upheaval surrounding him. Her thoughts also focused on Widkelly's birth family: had they survived?

Unlike Samantha, who had only recently been matched with her son and was anxiously waiting to receive approval to come to Haiti to meet him, Catherine had already met her daughter and was nearing the end of the adoption process. She was hoping that she would receive the news as early as summertime that she could bring her daughter home to France. It was around midnight in Paris when Catherine opened the email telling her about the earthquake, and she was immediately relieved to know that Nadége was safe. Catherine also saw several posts on Facebook from GLA staff members, offering her even more assurance that everyone was alive and well.

Catherine was relieved to know that everyone at GLA had survived the earthquake, so she decided to sleep, secure in the knowledge that her precious daughter was safe. She found sleep to be elusive, however, so she returned to her computer, searching the Internet for more information. The more news she saw, the more she realized the enormity of the quake and the gravity of the situation. Sleep was no longer an option. Learning more about what was happening in Haiti was all that mattered now.

Throughout the evening, more and more families in North America learned the news of what the children they were adopting had experienced only a few hours earlier in Haiti. In Florida, Charlie and Laura stumbled across news of the earthquake when they were online. They turned the television to a news station and began emailing anyone they thought might have information about GLA and the kids. It was not long before they saw a post that everyone at GLA was okay. This was reassuring, but they still had many concerns for GLA, and especially for their son, Wadson. They worried about supplies at GLA: would we have enough food and water? They also worried about how this disaster would impact their adoption. Wadson was already legally their son, and they had hoped that within a few months he would have the travel documents necessary for them to bring him home. Would it still be possible to get Wadson's passport and visa? Charlie and Laura kept the TV on and scoured the Internet for news, anxious to know as much as possible.

Farther north on the east coast, Jeff and Janet also learned about the earthquake through the Internet a few hours after it had happened. They were immediately concerned for GLA and the children, and were relieved when they saw the notice on GLA's website saying that everyone was okay. Knowing that this included their daughter, Rénalia, they felt immense relief as they switched the television to news coverage of the event. Friends and family called as they learned the news, and Jeff and Janet shared the little they knew with others who had the same questions they did. They accepted whatever comfort their friends and family had to offer, watched the GLA site for any updates, and prayed for Rénalia and all the others at GLA and in Haiti.

Edward and Sarah were one of the few families to hear about the earthquake directly from Haiti. After work, Sarah had run some errands with her daughter; they came home to a blinking light signaling a message on the answering machine. When she listened to the message, she heard the voice of a friend who was visiting GLA that week: "There's been an earthquake in Haiti. We are okay, we are with your boys, and they are okay, too."

Sarah was stunned by the news and uncertain what to think, but very thankful to know that at least the twins she and Edward were adopting were safe and were being cared for by good friends. Sarah flipped on the news for more information and began to recognize the true gravity of the situation. She was more relieved than ever to know that her friends and her sons had survived, but she worried about their safety in the coming days and weeks. What would happen if the supplies ran out and they couldn't get more? She also thought about the unfairness of the situation, that such a disaster should happen in Haiti, where people were least prepared for it. The nation often struggled under hurricanes, or floods, or droughts, or political upheaval, adding to the challenges of their already difficult lives. When would it ever end?

Sarah and Edward spent the evening watching the news and communicating with loved ones about the disaster. For many of their family members and friends, the earthquake offered a shocking view of the Haiti they had been unable to see and experience. They had a prior interest in the nation, especially since Sarah and Edward's daughter Angie had been adopted from GLA several years earlier, but their local news typically offered only occasional glimpses into anything happening in Haiti. Now they were getting a vivid picture of its landscape, its beauty and pain, and the widespread devastation caused by the earthquake.

Dawn arrived home late on January 12, having been out for much of the evening. Not long after she returned, her dad called, telling her about the earthquake. Dawn immediately went to GLA's website, where she saw the message that everyone was okay. Like so many of the other adoptive parents, it was only after Dawn knew that the children were safe that she searched for more information and began to understand the enormity of the disaster.

Dawn was thankful that her daughter, Naïka, and the rest of the children and staff had survived, but her relief was only partial. She had read on the GLA website that John had checked the buildings and had not found any cracks indicating structural damage, only those to the façade, but she worried about the possibility of invisible damage the building might have sustained. All she could do from her home in Michigan was pray for everyone's safety, which she did fervently.

Dawn also began to wonder what this would mean for her adoption. It had already been more than a year since she had been matched with her daughter, and the adoption process was moving slowly in Haiti. She feared this would mean another lengthy delay.

However, as Dawn continued to learn more about the extent of the damage to the Haitian government and their offices, she started wondering if it might not be possible for the kids to join their families with some sort of emergency status. Since the government issued emergency medical visas for people who needed medical care they could not receive in Haiti, could it be possible to get similar visas to allow the adoptive children to escape the disaster zone? Dawn didn't know the answer, but she hoped that it could be done, and she began calling and emailing others who might be able to help her figure it out.

Unlike the adoptive families in North America, who had learned about the earthquake and their children's safety before going to bed on the night of January 12, many of the European families had not. Because of the time difference, it was nearly eleven o'clock at night when the earthquake happened, so they woke up to the news on the morning of January 13.

Rik and Janka heard it on the early morning television news in the Netherlands. The more they saw, the more concerned they became about Haiti, GLA, and especially their son, Jephté. Needing to know more, Janka went to GLA's website, where she saw the posted notice. Jephté was okay! Soon the phone started ringing, as family and friends called to offer their sympathy and support. Everyone wanted to help out, but from so far away, they knew there was little they could do. Rik and Janka continued to watch news of the situation in Haiti and pray for the safety of Jephté and everyone else at GLA.

Sonja was already at work in Luxembourg, just ready to start the day, when her friend called her at the office. Through tears, Sonja's friend told her that she had heard terrible news about Haiti on the radio that morning. There had been an earthquake, and Port-au-Prince was badly damaged.

Sonja tried to look up information about the earthquake while also doing her work at the bank that morning. She was able to find some information about the earthquake, but because her work blocked many websites during working hours, she was not able to get onto GLA's website until lunch time, almost five hours later. Only then did she finally see the red-lettered text, calming her fears and assuring her that her son was alive and well, and that GLA's buildings had withstood the earthquake and were still strong.

Obviously, it was not only the adoptive families who were touched by the disaster in Haiti. They had the most personal interest in the lives of the children at GLA, but millions of others around the world had loved ones—both related and not—who had suffered through the earthquake. It was an anxious time for many as they awaited news, and that news was not always comforting.

CHAPTER 4

AWAKENING TO AWARENESS

But everything exposed by the light becomes visible,
for it is light that makes everything visible.

~ Ephesians 5:13–14a

BACK IN HAITI, MORNING'S LIGHT began to shine. Wednesday was a new day, but the horrors of the previous hours were more than just a nightmare; they were now our life. Nothing had changed overnight, and the few hours that had passed did little to prepare us for the challenges of this day and the many more that would follow it. We didn't know what to expect, as the tragedy had quickly been shrouded by the dark of night. This new day would bring an awareness of our true situation, of the fate of a nation. We dreaded the day and that knowledge, as if ignorance could change the truth.

There was an eerie stillness when I awoke early on the morning of January 13, or perhaps solemnity had taken over my spirit. I looked at the clock on the nightstand by my bed—6:00 a.m. I had slept only about four hours. Susan was not in the room when I woke up, but soon the door opened and she came back in. She told me that the nannies had brought the children inside about half an hour earlier. They had all spent the night outside in the cold winter air, huddled together under blankets to find as much warmth as possible. Susan was returning the children who had slept in our room to their nurseries as well. She had not slept much, if at all, during the night hours. She had been anxious for the children, frequently making rounds in the yard, as well as caring for the ones in our room. Atlanta needed to be fed every two hours through her feeding tube, and Darline also required fluids throughout the night. Even when Susan did lie down, her mind would not rest long enough for her body to sleep. I understood those emotions, but I was thankful that my body had not reacted the same way. I had been exhausted from shock and trauma, and my body had gone into protective mode. For a few precious hours, I had slept in blissful ignorance.

As Susan returned the children to their nurseries, two at a time, I stayed in the room with the others, preparing for the day ahead. I dressed as quickly as I could, taking no care for anything except comfort. I didn't know how long the day would last or what I would be required to face, and I wanted to be ready for whatever was to come. I was eager, if not to face the day, at least to get started doing whatever I could to help.

From inside my room it had seemed a gray day, as if even God in heaven was weeping over the destruction in Haiti. When I stepped outside, however, I saw that it was in fact a bright, sunny day, which was certainly better suited to help the thousands in Port-au-Prince searching for their loved ones, if not quite as accurate a reflection of my soul.

When I arrived in the office that morning, Dixie was already in the middle of a hundred tasks. While the rest of us had spent most of the night in our rooms, Dixie had not. She had stayed in the office, where she passed a sleepless night hard at work. Suddenly her orphanage was in the middle of a disaster zone, and it was a heavy responsibility. She was busy strategizing and preparing, as best she could, for what was to come. At one point, she had lain down on the couch in the living room, but she was only able to doze for about half an hour before she was back up again, her mind racing.

The first thing I did when I entered the office that morning was to ask Dixie how I could be most useful. The instant the earth first shook, my job changed. All of our jobs had changed. The day-to-day work we normally did was no longer significant, and we were all focused on one thing—keeping the orphanage running and doing whatever we could to keep everyone safe and alive.

Dixie gave me a slightly dazed look, as if she were so overwhelmed she didn't know where to begin. Quickly, though, she mentally prioritized the work she could delegate and named off a couple of tasks for me do. The first of these was to compile accurate and detailed information on our foreign visitors—North Americans and Europeans—who were at GLA. Names and home countries were easy, but I also needed passport numbers and hometowns to give to the respective embassies. It was another reminder of the scale of the disaster surrounding us: governments were trying to track down their citizens and account for their whereabouts. I started with the staff, families, and volunteers who were on site at the main house. When the visitors staying at the other houses arrived, some of them had their passports with them. Others had left them behind, but gave permission for our staff members to go through their bags to find them. It took several hours before I was able to collect the necessary information, communicating via Internet chat or face to face, since phone service was jammed.

The volunteers had come down to the main house, just as they did any normal morning, though they arrived earlier than usual on this day. Like the rest of us, they were weary, and it showed on their faces, but they were tough, and ready to face the challenges of the day. It had been a short night for them as well, with one of our staff members driving them back to the toddler house around 11:00 p.m., shortly after the children had all gone inside and before they had returned to spend the night in the yard. They had walked into the courtyard at the toddler house to the sound of the nannies praying and singing. The children were all inside, asleep, and the nannies who didn't need to be inside with them were in the courtyard. Some of the volunteers stayed and sang or just listened, joining in the spirit of the broken-hearted worship, while others went upstairs to their rooms for the chance to sleep. All had been deeply shaken by the events that had occurred.

When they arrived at the main house that next morning, their fatigue and worry showed on their faces. They had come to GLA to work with the children, though, and they recognized that we needed their help now more than ever. It was not long before the continuing aftershocks wore on the nannies' nerves and they returned outside with the children and volunteers. The collective group of adults cared for the needs of the children throughout the day.

The only children who were not outside in the courtyard were the NICU babies. They were the smallest and most fragile, and several of them required ongoing observation and medical attention. Susan had insisted they stay inside, and the NICU nannies stayed with her. They cared for the needs of their eleven children, providing as much love and comfort as they could, both to the children and to one another. Susan spent much of her time in that nursery, tending to the children's medical needs, but she also made frequent trips outside to assess the children in the front yard and to monitor their health. There had been a stomach virus going around the nurseries for the past few days, and sickness does not stop for disaster. Especially in these unusual circumstances, Susan wanted to ensure that the children were getting proper medical attention. Life tends to be more fragile in Haiti than in more developed countries. So many of the children have not had proper nutrition during the formative times of their growth and development, so they don't have the reserves of good health to fall back on when they get sick. We were used to seeing children who were apparently quite healthy in the morning turn critically ill by evening, and we had sometimes seen children die just as quickly. Susan was determined to do everything she could to keep all these children alive and healthy, a more challenging task in the midst of these unusual circumstances.

Not long after I arrived in the office, Laurie learned that missionary friends of ours were going down into Port-au-Prince to see first-hand what was happening in Haiti. Up to that point, our information had primarily come from CNN and Internet articles. Phone service was extremely limited, and we didn't know how reliable any of the word-of-mouth news was. Laurie asked to go along, not eager to see the devastation, but desperate to see and know the truth firsthand. Laurie had grown up in Haiti and had spent her teenage years visiting places which she had heard were now piles of rubble. She had to see it with her own eyes. Sometimes our imaginations and rumors are worse than the truth, but even when they are not, there is something solid, something valuable, about *knowing*. Our friends came to pick up Laurie, along with Stephanie and one of our volunteers, who had also asked to go.

With Laurie and Stephanie gone, I was alone in the office with Dixie. I spent much of my time doing whatever she asked of me, whatever needed done at that moment—a plate of food, messages taken to others, emails sent, photos labeled, finding information on-line; I helped in any way possible. It was less than twenty-four hours after the earthquake, and we were still in a state of urgent disaster relief. Life felt completely out of control, and it was hard to imagine it ever being anything like normal again.

Not surprisingly, I had received many emails from adoptive families overnight, all wanting to hear from us that their kids were okay. Knowing that Dixie would be busy and that I was the one who usually corresponded with them anyway, the families contacted me. I responded to each of them, not in detail, but assuring them that we had survived the night and that everyone was safe. I tried to recall personal accounts of the children whenever possible, reassuring the parents not only that their children were physically unharmed, but that they were also doing well emotionally.

From the time I first logged onto my computer, which had finally finished the hated back-up sometime after the earthquake the night before, I was bombarded by people wanting to know how I was doing, and how GLA was doing. It was a repeat of the night before in the hours after the earthquake. As more people were learning of the tragedy, more people needed our reassurances. My own family and friends were trying to contact me, as well as the family members of fellow GLA staff or others in Haiti. I also received messages from GLA supporters and friends wanting to assure us of their love and prayers. On that first morning, with everything in such a rush and with no extra time, I didn't even bother to capitalize my words as I typed. I know that will sound trivial to some people, but considering that at the time I used proper capitalization and no abbreviations even in text messages, it was significant. It seems ridiculous that taking the time to press the shift button was a bother, but on that day, it truly was. Anything that wasn't absolutely necessary was a waste of our time and valuable energy.

The Internet was our lifesaver at that time, our connection both with our co-workers half a mile up the mountain and with those outside of Haiti and around the world. What we were just starting to learn was that we were one of the few places in Haiti that still had Internet access and satellite phone service, which is perhaps why our phone was constantly ringing. News media from around the world wanted to cover the story in Haiti, and they wanted to talk to those who were there. Once word got out that we were accessible and willing to talk, our phones rang constantly with calls from major news organizations: NBC, Fox News, CNN, the BBC, and others. Dixie could not even set the phone back in the cradle at the completion of one call before it would ring again with another. This happened more than once that day, and I think nearly every one of us did at least one interview—even the volunteers and visiting families!

Those interviews were hard on all of us: talking through our situation made it more real, in some ways even more so than living it.

The disaster we found ourselves in was far too big for us to handle on our own, though. We needed outside help for both GLA and the nation of Haiti. Being from Scotland, Susan knew that she was one of only a handful of British citizens in the country. She also knew that people back in Great Britain would be more likely to respond to hearing a familiar accent, that it would make the situation more real to them. Susan recognized that we needed the help and she could do something about getting it, for us and for Haiti.

Susan's first interview was in the early morning hours, shortly after midnight. Dixie had called to her and, with a pleading look in her eye, asked if Susan would please speak with the BBC reporters. She didn't pressure Susan to take the call, telling her she understood if she could not do it, but it was obvious that Dixie felt alone with the burden. Doing those interviews was especially difficult for Susan, as she usually tried to stay in the background and away from public attention. Talking to news reporters was close to her worst nightmare, yet she recognized the need for publicity. Susan took the phone, thinking of her family back home in Scotland. With the difference in time zones, it was early morning and they would be waking up soon and hearing about the earthquake for the first time. Susan was worried what they would hear, and she didn't want them wondering if she had survived and fearful of her situation. She did that interview in the hope it would reach her family and reassure them. In fact, when her family at home heard the news of the earthquake, they first heard an interview with Dixie, whom they knew to be Susan's boss, and the very next thing they heard was Susan's own voice, so they received the assurance she wanted for them.

After that first call, the BBC called again and again, wanting to talk to Dixie and to Susan. During those days most of us did whatever was necessary, even when our tasks were unpleasant or not something we wanted to do. We did what we knew needed to be done; we did what was best for the orphanage and the children. We desperately needed help, and we hoped those interviews would touch hearts and bring us the aid required.

I didn't do nearly as many interviews as Dixie and Susan, but I did take one that first day. At one point, I was in Dixie's office and saw that she had a Skype interview scheduled with one of my local news stations. I commented on that fact, and Dixie suggested that maybe I could talk to them instead. She was long past tired of talking to people, and she thought they might be interested in connecting with an area resident working in Haiti. I knew that, compared to the news blitz Dixie was facing, an interview or two was not a big burden for me and it was a relief for her.

Many of the media outlets Dixie spoke to wanted pictures, and she asked me to email the ones we had to the news agencies. As crazy as the night before had been, I had done little more than dump the pictures onto the computer and send them to Jean at GLA's Colorado office. Dixie had labeled and sent a few photos out during the long night hours, but most still needed to be organized and properly filed. I knew these were unusual times and that we would want photos in the future, although we still didn't realize just how historic this disaster would turn out to be. I organized and labeled the photos as best I could and sent them on to media agencies around the world.

All day long I was restless, unable to focus or concentrate on any one thing for more than a few minutes. My mind was racing with all the tasks needing to be done, and I struggled to prioritize them. I did my best to complete whatever task I was working on, but usually I was interrupted at least two or three times by other urgent tasks that needed my immediate attention. I took frequent breaks to visit the children outside—comforting them for their sakes, holding them for mine. I tried to encourage the volunteers, most of whom still had shell-shocked expressions on their faces.

On one of my visits, I looked around at the children, playing in the morning sunshine. *They're outside!* I thought, an obvious deduction since I myself was outside, and I knew they had been there for several hours. *They need hats!* was my next logical thought. It was an orphanage rule that when the children were in the sun on the balcony for a long time or went for walks in the neighborhood, they needed to wear hats to shield their eyes and protect their skin. Intent on my task, I ran upstairs to the balcony where I knew the hats were kept.

When I opened the door to the balcony, I was immediately distracted by the beauty of the mountains across from me. The grandeur of the mountains in the crystal clear air stopped me in my tracks. My tense muscles relaxed. The view from the volunteers' balcony on the third floor is truly breathtaking, and nearly every visitor comments on it the first time he or she steps through the door. Across the valley, the mountains rise into the sky. Sometimes they are shrouded in clouds, while at other times only a mist dances along the top of them, hiding the peaks. On a cloudless day, they glint green in the sun's full light, covered with deep shadows in the morning or evening. The mountains in front of me that day were crisp and clear, with sharply defined lines. They were majestic; they were calm. Most significantly, they were unaffected by the chaos and tragedy playing out in front of them. They were as beautiful as ever, and in that moment they were infinitely reassuring to me.

It was a comfort to stop for a few brief moments, sit down, and take in the panorama. My view of Port-au-Prince and the disaster there was blocked by mountains behind me, and all around there was only peace and beauty. It was the first touch of healing that had been breathed into my soul since the earthquake. I sat and absorbed the beauty for only a couple of minutes, but it revived my soul. It gave me the strength to go on just a little longer.

My mind was too unsettled to rest long, though. I soon returned downstairs to deliver the children's hats to the nannies and to return to the work that was awaiting me in the office.

Throughout the morning, whenever Dixie had a few moments of peace from the phone calls (usually when someone else was on the line being interviewed), different nannies would come to her, asking permission to go home and see what was left of their lives, their families, and their homes. Only a few had been able to reach loved ones on their cell phones or had family or friends arrive at our gates with news. The nannies wanted to learn what had become of their world. Dixie was sympathetic, denying no one's request lightly, but she was unable to let everyone go. None of the nannies who were supposed to start their shift that morning had come to work. We didn't know if it was a choice they made, if they were unable to find transportation, or if they had been injured or killed by the earthquake. As much as Dixie understood the need of these women to go to their families, we had nearly 100 children in the nurseries needing their attention. Whenever Dixie granted permission, it was with instructions to go, check out the circumstances, and come back as soon as possible so that someone else could also go. Whenever Dixie denied permission, it was with the explanation that there were not enough ladies currently at the house and that everyone would be able to leave as soon as the staffing situation allowed.

We also had many visitors at God's Littlest Angels that day. As not all of the children in our care were true orphans, their biological families would sometimes visit. Immediately following the earthquake, many of them came to see the children they had given up. They hadn't come to take them away—if anything, they were more determined than ever that their children should have the lives that they could not provide—but they wanted to see them, hold them, and know that they had survived this great tragedy that had come to Haiti. The same love that had enabled them to give their children the hope of a better life than they could provide in their uncertain future, now compelled them to come to their children following the earthquake. They needed to see with their own eyes that their children had survived. It seemed that every time I walked through the visiting room, there were two or three families there, the parents holding their children tightly in their arms.

Some foreigners who have been to Haiti might suppose that it is easy for Haitian parents to give their children up for adoption. After all, on my first weeklong visit several years earlier, I lost track of how many parents offered me their children as I walked through rural villages. However, it is simply not true that Haitian parents are heartless, that they give up their children because they do not care. The simple truth is that most parents give up their children *because* of their love, not from a lack of it. They know their lives, they know Haiti, and they know the odds against their child having a good, healthy life. It is often a sacrificial love, a love that is willing to give up that child in the hope that he or she will have more in life than the parents will be able to give. Many parents regularly visited their children in the orphanage. After the children have left Haiti—and presumably also the parents' lives—many parents continue to return, asking for pictures and any available information about them. One of our favorite events was when a newly united adoptive family was able to meet with their child's biological family. It was a special experience, a time of love and sorrow, and a chance for all of them (with the help of a translator) to share their hopes and dreams for the child. It was a time for the adoptive family to see their child's past and an opportunity for the biological family to glimpse their child's future.

Meanwhile, in the yard outside, the children continued to enjoy life, largely unaffected by the tragedy playing out around them. They were being loved, they were being cared for, and they were unaware of how precarious our lives had become. Instead, they simply enjoyed the beautiful day and the opportunity to be outside. After feeding the children their simple lunch of rice, the nannies lined the children up on the blankets and laid them down for their naps. Once this was done, many of the nannies huddled themselves into the back of the same pick-up trucks where they had found shelter the night before. Most of the children slept; a few of the older, more adventurous ones stayed awake, but for the most part they sat quietly, playing with their toys. The volunteers stayed with the children in groups of two or three, the others taking advantage of the chance for a well-deserved and much-needed break and the opportunity to communicate with loved ones at home.

CHAPTER 5

THE STATE OF HAITI AND GLA

The LORD is my rock, my fortress and my deliverer,
my God is my rock, in whom I take refuge.
He is my shield and the horn of my salvation, my stronghold.

~ Psalm 18:2

NOT SURPRISINGLY, JANUARY 13 FELT like the day after a disaster. In many ways we were still in shock, functioning on a sort of protective autopilot, living each individual moment in the hope of surviving that minute, that hour, that day. In spite of the evidence to the contrary, it was still inconceivable to us that the scenes we were now acting out were, in fact, our lives. We felt disbelief and a strong sense of unreality, because the world we were living in had suddenly become unfamiliar and foreign. We felt as if were no longer living in the same world we had always known.

This tragedy, like all disasters, was something that belonged on the pages of a newspaper or a television story about people far away, not happening to people like us. We were now those people far away whom others around the world were watching. Still, we knew without a doubt that what we were experiencing was real; we knew we were in the middle of something much bigger than ourselves. So, as much as possible, we pushed our emotions to the side, knowing they threatened to incapacitate us, to send us into hiding in our rooms or sobbing with grief. We chose to act with our minds and our hands, rather than listen to our hearts and emotions.

Overwhelmed does not even begin to describe how we felt: we were powerless. We had no sense of a future, no hope that things would soon be better or return to normal. The only time that existed was that very moment. In the morning, evening seemed an impossible lifetime away. Each night, we fell asleep, knowing we would wake in the morning to begin the process again. There was no way around the life that had been thrust upon us, so we did our best to struggle through it.

Much of what we were experiencing was from what is commonly referred to as the "Haiti earthquake," the one measuring 7.0 that occurred at 4:53 p.m. on January 12, 2010. That earthquake had lasting implications on our lives, but these emotions and fears were compounded when that was not the end. The ground did not violently shake, but then settle back to its usual calm with maybe a stray aftershock or two. Instead, aftershocks of all varieties continued with disconcerting and unpredictable regularity. By 11:30 a.m., just over eighteen hours after the initial quake, we saw a report that more than forty aftershocks had been recorded in Haiti. However, that counted only those aftershocks measuring 4.5 or higher, and we felt many, many more than that. It was a rare occasion when a span of ten minutes passed without a notable aftershock. The constant shaking did nothing to soothe our rattled nerves. Rather, it brought us to the brink of mental breakdown.

Being from the Midwest, where the ground generally stays where it belongs, I quickly learned that my experiences did not match any expectations of earthquakes that I had previously formed. I had thought of rumbling and shaking, of jarring and jerking that would knock you around and toss things to the ground. That was all true, but it was only part of the story. Earthquakes are not one-size-fits-all, and there is nothing standard or predictable about them. It was as if the earth were a living, breathing thing that was writhing in pain and wanted to make sure we suffered along with it.

Each time the earth began to shake, our bodies were instantly tense and alert. Some of the aftershocks lasted several seconds and increased in intensity, causing us to fear that they would grow into something truly terrifying. Even the shortest aftershocks—the ones that were over before we had a chance to respond—ignited this fear. We never knew if the next shock would follow immediately or if it would be several minutes later—the only thing that seemed certain was that another aftershock would come. This stress only added to the exhaustion we were already feeling.

As frequent as the aftershocks were, they were not constant. What was constant was a sense of motion, of rocking. The day after the earthquake, this motion was so violent that I struggled to write on a piece of paper sitting on my desk. My head, my hand, and even the desk were each being rocked differently, and it was a challenge to coordinate all three. To a lesser extent this rocking motion contin-ued at least through the first week. It was strong enough that many of us experienced motion sickness simply from sitting at our desks. Several of my co-workers took anti-nausea medicine when the rocking became too difficult or prolonged.

At one point on Wednesday afternoon, Dixie discovered another measure of the earth's continued motion. As she stood in the doorway to her office with her hands on the doorframe on either side of her, she could feel the frame moving subtly from side to side. The movement was imperceptible to our eyes, but easily felt.

Another unexpected occurrence was that we sometimes experienced the motion through a sudden wave of dizziness. One of the things I learned is that there is directionality to earthquakes. They feel stronger or weaker depending on where a person is located and in which direction he is facing. Where one person might feel the motion, another might have a sense of being suddenly dizzy and lightheaded, without actually feeling the motion.

However, what became the most frequent manifestation of the earth's movement was simply vibration. It felt as though someone nearby was operating a jackhammer, and we could feel the vague rumblings. As I sat at my desk, I could feel the motion through my feet, through the seat and back of my chair, and through my arms resting on my desk. We knew that there was no escape—nowhere to go that was still.

Most disconcerting of all, we felt the earth's movement when we were lying down. I am sure there is a scientific explanation about surface area and exposure to the rocking, but none of that meant anything to us and our unsettled nerves. Being constantly reminded of the motion felt like a violation of our privacy, of our opportunity to rest. We tried to convince our overstressed bodies to relax enough that we could sleep. Several weeks after the earthquake, I noticed that I had developed the habit of shaking my own bed as I lay down each night. It seemed an odd thing to do until I realized that this was actually a defense mechanism on my part. If my bed was going to be shaking, I wanted to believe that I was the one causing it, not the elusive and hated tectonic plates.

Much of our unrest and tattered nerves were due not so much to the hundreds of jarring, never-ending aftershocks, but to the constant rocking we experienced. We prayed for the ground to be still and to feel peace, but it didn't happen on that day or for many more to come.

Late on Wednesday afternoon—the day after our nightmare had begun—Laurie and the others returned from Port-au-Prince with pictures and stories of the horrors they had seen. As much as our minds sought to understand the situation and learn how our beloved Haiti had fared, we were also afraid to do so, knowing there was only so much we could bear. As it turned out, however, they didn't want to tell us the stories any more than we wanted to hear them. It did not seem possible, but in many ways the situation was even worse than what we had previously heard.

I didn't want to see Laurie's pictures of the devastation, but I had no choice: it was my job. One of my responsibilities (before the earthquake) had been to take and organize all GLA photos. Now, that had transitioned into distributing photos to the various media outlets who had been interviewing us throughout the day. They wanted pictures of what was happening in Haiti, and I was responsible to send them, no matter how abhorrent sorting through them might be.

The pictures of Port-au-Prince were every bit as awful as I had imagined they would be. They were things that no one should ever have to see, much less experience. Laurie had not been trying to take graphic or sensational pictures; she simply took pictures of what she saw, pictures of the city and its streets. She didn't take half the photos she could have, and she had deliberately avoided photographing scenes that were disrespectful or gruesome. Even so, the photos I saw were more than enough to justify my desire to avoid them.

I had not wanted to see the pictures of devastated Haiti for the same reasons I hadn't wanted to go into town, into the worst of the disaster. Part of my reluctance was denial. If I did not actually *see* the devastation, then I could still deceive myself and believe that the situation was not as horrible as I knew it must be. Another reason was simply self-protection. In those days, it took all our strength and emotional energy just to survive. I knew that if I were to truly comprehend the magnitude of the disaster we were living through, it would debilitate me, and I had no time for that. We did not have the luxury of grief, especially in those first hours and days.

Many of Laurie's pictures were simply of the physical damage the earthquake had caused: fallen buildings, crushed cars, and streets filled with the rubble of broken houses. Other photos showed the impact of the earthquake on human life. Dead bodies lined the streets. The bodies had been covered in tarps and blankets, but their feet were sticking out, sometimes revealing the crushing wounds they had received. Family members were doing their best to remove the bodies of loved ones, carrying them away on makeshift stretchers so they could give the bodies a respectful good-bye. There was blood in the streets that day, running like water. Even seeing the fallen and collapsed buildings was emotional, knowing that people were trapped inside, and that many of them would never make it out alive.

As much as we wanted to help Haiti on a larger scale, we knew that would be too much for us: the need was too great. There was nothing we could do for the masses suffering and hurting in Port-au-Prince; instead, we had to remain focused on our own survival.

The children in our care had always been our priority, and the disaster did not change that. Their birth families had been unable to support them, and they had entrusted them to us. The implicit promise was that we would make sure they had the best opportunities in life. These same children now had anxious and frightened adoptive families around the world. These families knew that their children, already a part of their families in their hearts, were suddenly in the middle of one of the most devastating natural disasters in history. They were fearful for their children's lives and uncertain about the future of their adoptions. We felt the burden and the responsibility of the trust that both the biological and adoptive families had placed in us.

When the rest of the staff from the toddler and guesthouses came to the main house for dinner, we had the first of what quickly became daily staff debriefings. So much was happening so quickly that we needed to regularly touch base regarding what was going on at all the different locations and to make sure everyone had all the necessary information. That first day, scarcely twenty-four hours after the first earthquake had, quite literally, shaken our world, we gathered together in the office, all of us in the same place for the first time since the disaster. Everyone was visibly tired, stressed, and worn from the eternal-seeming day we had just experienced.

Shortly before the meeting started, the phone rang yet again. I picked it up and looked at the caller ID before handing it to Dixie. "It's NBC," I told her, then had to laugh at myself and the crazy world I was living in. Within a single day, it had become commonplace for us to receive phone calls from major news organizations!

Dixie wrapped up the interview as the last staff members entered the office. We spent a few minutes talking through the events of the past day and the situations we were facing at each of the GLA locations. One of the most important things we discussed that day was our supply situation. The unavoidable truth is that disasters always produce shortages, and Haiti is a place where shortages are already a problem. Even in the best of times, our supplies were unpredictable.

Without a national or community water service, we bought our water from a local provider, who brought us several truckloads a week to store in our cisterns. During my eighteen months at GLA, there had been several times when we had depleted the cistern, or come close, before we were able to get more. Although those previous shortages had lasted only a few hours, it was always disconcerting to have no water. Gasoline and diesel fuel were also often in short supply. We would hear rumors that there was only a limited supply of diesel remaining in Haiti, and no one seemed to know quite when the next freighter would arrive bringing more. In general, medicines and food were less of an issue for us. While we were not always able to find exactly what we wanted at the stores, we kept our depots well stocked so that we would have what we needed, even if the stores did not.

We didn't know how our friends and suppliers had fared. Was the diesel company still standing? Had the water company's well, buildings, and trucks survived? And would they choose to bring *us* supplies, out of the tens of thousands of people who must be needing them? GLA had 152 children and infants to care for, as well as dozens of Haitian and foreign staff and visitors. Now we were faced with the possibility of running out of necessities. How were we going to survive?

As of January 13, the day after the earthquake, we had enough fuel to provide electricity for a few days, water for about a week and rice to last about a month. However, we were low on cooking oil for the rice and low on propane to heat the stove. We were well stocked with baby supplies such as diapers and formula, but with so many children, we knew we would need more soon.

No one dared to voice it aloud, but one of our greatest fears was that it would not be enough. We were afraid we would run out of supplies and be forced to watch the children suffer and die. Many of us would willingly have given up our rations for the children, but we knew that even that would not ensure their survival. So many of the children had been sick and malnourished before coming to GLA and were simply not as healthy as we were. It was the children who would suffer soonest and most.

Since we didn't know if we would be able to get more of any of these necessities, we did our best to conserve them and make sure they lasted as long as possible. We ate simply: plain rice without the usual meat, sauce, or other sides. As much as possible, those of us who had other sources of food tried to eat that and leave our portions for the children and the Haitian staff. Several of us had just been home for the Christmas holiday and had returned stocked with snacks and favorite foods from home. We were now especially thankful for these foods, as every little bit had become significant.

We had to use water to drink and to cook our food, but we did our best to limit it for other uses. We avoided flushing the toilet until absolutely necessary, used sanitizer instead of washing our hands, and didn't shower or do laundry, except for the necessary children's clothes, which were washed by hand to save water. Personal hygiene quickly became a low priority, and there was no time for vanity, even if we were talking with reporters via Skype. Under normal circumstances we only showered every other day and, unfortunately for me, on the night of the earthquake I was already overdue for a shower and washing my hair. It would be many days before we had enough water to shower again. I started wearing bandanas every day to hide the nastiness in my hair, at least as much as possible.

We were also concerned about our shortage of diesel fuel for the generators, as they were the source of all our electricity. Haitian electricity was unreliable under the best of circumstances and non-existent after the earthquake. Not only did we use electricity for the obvious things, such as lights, computers, and the Internet (which was our primary connection to the outside world), but also to run medical equipment for sick children and for the refrigerators and freezers which held our precious food supplies. Several of us started keeping cell phones and laptops charged at all times in preparation for a total loss of power. We also needed diesel fuel for the cars that we were using to search for supplies, as well as transporting staff members to and from their homes.

It is impossible to adequately express in words how we felt in those days. I can say that it was an uncertain time, that we did not know what to expect or what was going to happen next, but that doesn't come close to describing the fear—sometimes the terror and panic—we constantly felt. Our whole world had suddenly become un-stable and unpredictable—down to the very foundation of the earth. After the short staff meeting that evening, there was a time of prayer in place of our normal Wednesday night Bible study. Before it started, I went upstairs to see the kids, and while I was in the Urgence A nursery the house shook with another aftershock. At that point I experienced my first sensation of true panic. In that instant, I was certain the house was going to fall and we were all going to die. Not only that, I was powerless to do anything about it. I wasn't worried about that particular aftershock: it was already over. But others would come, and one of them would knock the house down. How could our building *not* fall, with everything it was experiencing?

I felt suffocated, short of breath, and desperate to be outside. I went down the back staircase that led through the kitchen to the nannies' sleeping quarters in the basement and outside to the laun-dry area in the back of the house. I couldn't go through the front living room where they were praying, I could *not* stay inside, and I didn't want to answer any questions about why I wasn't coming to the prayer service, or somehow be forced into staying. I needed space, and it was too claustrophobic inside. Even if they were praying.

Instead, I went to my room, which was somehow in my mind dissociated from the earthquake. It felt safer, anyhow, perhaps be-cause I had not spent much time in there over the past day and it had been my refuge from the troubles of the night before. My panic subsided, and I spent time in solitary prayer, which calmed my mind and my spirit.

That night, the second night, I was afraid to go to sleep. I was afraid an aftershock would come during the night, knock down our buildings, and I would never wake up. I knew that I needed sleep, needed it desperately to make it through the days ahead—assuming I lived that long—but how could I sleep?

I was tired: emotionally and physically exhausted. My body needed rest, but it was too much on guard to let down enough to sleep. It was a vicious circle; one I didn't know how to stop. Maybe I prayed. In those days it felt as if every breath was a prayer, a petition to the Almighty for the strength to go on just a little longer. I remembered a verse that had been meaningful to me in college, one that I had copied down and brought with me to Haiti. I found the paper with Psalm 4:8 printed on it: "I will lie down and sleep in peace for you alone, O Lord, make me dwell in safety." I propped the verse on my nightstand as a reminder to me, and it became my bedtime prayer each night. All of life is in God's hands, and it is His decision whether or not I wake up the next day. The earthquake was not the random event it seemed, and I took comfort in that fact.

We had survived another day. Each day behind us meant that the earthquake was farther in our past. Our hope was that each day would get a little easier than the one before until some future day—as impossible as it seemed at the time—when our lives would no longer be in chaos. We craved the routine existence we had so taken for granted. We knew that the lives we had known before were forever gone, but we hoped for a new life and a new routine that would one day be just as familiar to us as the old had been. We were one day closer to the fulfillment of that hope.

CHAPTER 6

IN OUR TIME OF NEED

Give us each day our daily bread.

~ Luke 11:3

ONE OF THE THINGS THAT kept us strong in the days immediately following the earthquake was the prayer and emotional support we received from family, friends, and even strangers from around the world. As difficult as those days were, we could sense that we were being upheld by a force stronger than ourselves. I do not claim to understand the mystery of prayer or how it works in people's lives; what I do know is that we could physically feel the peace and sustaining grace brought about by others' prayers on our behalf. We were helpless to do anything about our circumstances, and the people around the world avidly watching the news of Haiti were in most ways even more helpless. Separated by insurmountable obstacles that prevented them from helping us directly, and with no ability to physically lighten our burdens, they turned to God in prayer. Those prayers upheld us during that time. God heard their prayers and He acted.

One of our most immediate and urgent needs was childcare for all the children, especially the babies. Those nannies who had heard from their families were anxious to go to them. There was almost always bad news—their house was damaged or destroyed, loved ones injured, neighbors killed—and they longed to join their grieving and suffering families. Those who had not been able to get in touch with anyone from home were even more anxious to leave and learn the fate of family, friends, and neighbors. They were stuck in uncertainty, hoping for the best but fearing the worst. As Dixie allowed the staff to return home, a few at a time, we came to rely heavily on the volunteers who were with us.

Typically, our volunteers provided supplemental care and play time for the children outside of their nurseries. The nannies cared for the children, loved them, and attended to their basic needs, while the volunteers worked with the kids one-on-one, giving them special attention and working toward developmental milestones. They gave them the personal attention that was difficult to give in the large group setting of the nursery. This was the understanding our volunteers had when they arrived, and this was what they had signed up for. After the earthquake, however, our volunteers stepped up and took on new levels of childcare. Like the rest of us, they were willing to do whatever they could to keep things running as smoothly as possible.

In those first few days, the kids spent much of their time outdoors. The nannies were skittish and nervous with all the aftershocks we were experiencing. Every time the house would shake, the ladies would scream and run for the door. As soon as the shaking stopped, they moved outside with the children they were responsible for. Any time they could be convinced to move inside, it only lasted until the next aftershock, which was never far away. After the first night, Dixie insisted that the children stay inside overnight, but we all accepted that they were going to be outside during the days, including naptime.

A contributing factor to the nannies' reluctance to remain inside was the radio reports being broadcast at that time. They were cautioning people against returning to their homes and going into buildings, in the fear that they might fall in another aftershock. These reports were aimed at the large number of people in and around Port-au-Prince who were surrounded by massive destruction and where a large number of the buildings still standing were heavily damaged and in serious danger of falling. There was a general lack of understanding about earthquakes among the Haitian people, and some of them were returning to homes and shelters that were in precarious condition and could easily fall during the next strong aftershock. These reports were not particularly relevant to our staff, though, since our buildings had stood strong and had not lost any structural integrity, but we had a difficult time convincing them of that. The nannies preferred to stay outside, choosing even to sleep outside once the children had been settled and the night staff had taken over their care. Fortunately, Haiti's tropical climate allows for outdoor living, although January's chill made blankets and sweaters necessary.

During the day, when the kids were outside, we spread blankets on the concrete to provide a safer place for them to play. They became dirty, but we didn't have the water to spare to do laundry. We reasoned that dirty blankets were better than not using anything, and we did our best to keep them clean. Thankfully, it was the dry season and it didn't rain, because we did not have tarps or shelters.

Our yard was not designed as a childcare area, but the nannies and volunteers did a good job of supervising the kids and making sure they stayed in safe areas and kept out of trouble. The children wore hats, and we tried to keep them in shady areas as much as possible.

After the first day or two, many of the nannies were willing to return inside. Like the rest of us, they still found the aftershocks unsettling, but they were beginning to believe it was safe to stay in the buildings. Susan arranged shifts for the volunteers, ensuring the nurseries were all staffed and the children adequately cared for. The two youngest nurseries needed support from the volunteers because they didn't have enough nannies. Dixie asked the rest of the volunteers, those who were not assigned to a nursery, to each take five kids from the main nursery to the upstairs balcony. They were responsible for all childcare of those children throughout the day. That left the main nursery with a reasonable number of children for the nannies present.

It was a good system, and it worked, but it put a heavy and challenging load on our volunteers. They arrived around 7:00 a.m. to help feed the children breakfast, and then worked through dinner at 6:00 p.m., even staying to help bathe the children and prepare them for bed afterwards. They stopped only for short breaks so they themselves could get a quick bite to eat and a bit of rest while the kids were napping. They were working eleven to twelve hours a day, actively engaged in watching the children: feeding, changing diapers, stopping temper tantrums, enforcing safety rules, keeping the peace, comforting fussy or scared children, and kissing scrapes when necessary. They worked hard to ensure the kids felt safe, loved, and secure, especially in light of everything that was going on around them.

The earth's movement didn't bother the young children as much as the fear and uncertainty they sensed in the trusted adults in their world. Their neatly structured routine had been thrown off, and when things didn't quickly return to normal, they didn't know how to respond. They watched the responses and emotions of the adults around them. In spite of their own fears and concerns, the volunteers tried to provide security for the babies. Those volunteers were in many ways our heroes in the first days after the earthquake. With so many of our nannies not there, it was such a blessing to know that the children were still being well cared for. With so much chaos going on all around us, it was one less thing to worry about.

Our volunteers accepted their new roles, willingly working long hours to help us and to care for the children, but the strain was a lot for them to take. They had been through the same trauma of actually experiencing the earthquake that the rest of us had, but they were in a strange and unfamiliar place. Not one of our volunteers had been in Haiti for even a full week at the time of the first earthquake. Nine of the eleven had arrived since Sunday, four of them arriving in Haiti and at GLA on Tuesday, mere hours before the earthquake. We knew that them being there was an answer to an unasked prayer, but it was a challenge for them. Most of them had never been to Haiti before, and they were still trying to adjust to the unfamiliar culture. Even before the earthquake, Haiti was one of the poorest nations in the world and visiting there, especially for the first time, was often a startling and eye-opening experience.

It quickly became obvious that the stress and long hours were wearing on the volunteers. They needed a break. After several days, we were organized enough to institute a more sustainable system of dividing the volunteers into two teams who worked separate shifts. The first group came early to help with breakfast and worked through until right before dinner. The second group came later in the morning and worked until the kids were in bed for the night. That way we were able to keep the nursery staffed and to provide the nannies with the support they needed but without burning out our volunteers.

For those of us who lived in Haiti, our burdens were different. We were familiar with the country, the poverty, the way of life. We had willingly given up our lives at home out of love for the island nation and its people. Haiti had, at some point, become home to each one of us, occupying a very special place in our lives and our hearts. Then, on January 12, our home and our hearts were broken. We experienced the earthquake, which was traumatic enough, but what was even more disturbing was the fact that we had a fairly clear picture of what this would mean for the people of Haiti. We felt, to varying degrees, the weight of responsibility for our 152 children, Haitian staff, and foreign visitors. We had friends and loved ones—people we cared about—whose safety and futures were suddenly unsure. The burden was too heavy; all of us knew that we would never be able to care for all the needs in Haiti or even just our little corner of it. Those of us living and working at GLA were overwhelmed. It was with unspeakable gratitude that we witnessed the outpouring of support and aid from the international community. We needed them desperately, and the response was so much more than any of us could have hoped or imagined.

The night of the earthquake we had felt completely isolated and alone. We were used to Haiti being largely ignored or misrepresented by the news media. The stories typically reported violence, rioting, disorder, and despair. Those stories are a part of Haiti, but by no means the whole picture. There is also beauty, hope, love, and sacrifice. The everyday struggles of the Haitian people were largely ignored by Western media, and the sensational stories that did make the news only inspired fear. We had not expected things to be any different now.

We saw our needs and our own inability to provide for those needs. The infrastructure of Haiti had been destroyed, telephones and communication were severely crippled, at least one grocery store had been flattened and we didn't yet know the condition of the few others. Even if all the other stores and warehouses were undamaged, though, how long would their supplies last among so many hungry people? How long would it be until they could replenish their stock? Nearly everything in Haiti was imported, but the port had sunk into the bay, and we didn't know how long it would be until they could get more supplies from the Dominican Republic on the other side of the island. We envisioned that the supplies that had survived in Haiti were all that would be available for some time to come, and that hundreds of thousands of people would be fighting over the same few goods.

We sat in uncertainty. The obvious reaction would have been to panic, but I don't believe that any of us did. We were aware of our situation, and we did what we could to try to procure supplies. Still, we knew that much of it was out of our control. We had so many other urgent tasks requiring our attention and care that we didn't have the time or energy to worry about things we could do nothing to change. We knew that we were utterly incapable of providing for our own needs and those of the children in our care. Matthew

6:34 says, "Therefore do not worry about tomorrow . . . Each day has enough trouble of its own." We began to live this verse, not out of faith as much as out of desperation and powerlessness. It was not that our faith in God was so great—although we had seen Him provide in times of shortage previously—but because we had no choice. We were completely in His hands. Whether we were guided by the right motives or not, God proved Himself to be more than faithful. The idea of God as provider is one of those truths that is commonly accepted but rarely experienced in the Western world. Now, for the first time in many of our lives, we were fully dependent on God's provision—literally for our daily bread. It was amazing to see His hand at work, caring for us and providing for our needs.

It was God who provided, but it was also exciting to see who responded to His call to be His hands and feet in our time of need. Those were some of our most indescribable, emotional, and heartwarming experiences in the days following the traumatic earthquake. We received the first donation of physical supplies at GLA early Friday morning, only two and a half days after the initial earthquake. Missionaries from the Dominican Republic had heard about our plight and wanted to help. They would have arrived sooner, but were understandably cautious about driving through a disaster-ridden Port-au-Prince too late at night with a truckload of supplies. The situation had generally remained calm, and there had not yet been rioting, but as time went on the people's situation would worsen, and there was no need to see what desperate people might be willing to do. The missionaries spent Thursday night camped outside the city and arrived at GLA early Friday morning. We had heard that they were coming but were afraid to hope: afraid something would happen to delay them or that they would never make it. To actually see them first thing the next morning brought relief, joy, and hope, knowing that we now had provisions for a little bit longer.

They might have looked like ordinary men bringing a couple drums of diesel, some water, and simple food supplies, but to us they were so much more. They were God's messengers sent with provisions, a reminder that God knew our needs, that He cared and that He would provide in his own way and time, not ours. They apologized for not bringing more, but they had already given us a gift whose worth we could not express, as much as we might try. They will never know just how much their gift meant to us. They cannot understand, unless they have been in the same position.

I interacted with our benefactors only briefly on my way into the office that morning as they dropped off their gifts and immediately returned home. I stopped when I saw them, overcome with gratitude and humbled by the generosity of strangers. Tears threatened to spill from my eyes and all I could say was a simple "thank you." It was such an inadequate expression of my heart, but no words could truly convey my thoughts. I quickly fled inside before my emotions could get the best of me. These strangers' gift of compassion touched a broken part of my soul.

We needed the physical supplies they brought. Those provisions would provide for our needs for a few more days. Living as we were from day to day, it was a comfort to know that we had what we needed even for such a short while longer. It reminded me of Elijah and the widow who had no extra oil, yet it never ran out. God didn't give us more than we needed, but just enough. As much as we needed their supplies, however, the hope they brought was equally valuable. It was not so much that we had lost our hope as that we were exhausted. Our responsibilities were overwhelming, and we were fighting so hard to simply survive. To know that there were other people out there willing to help, willing to share our burden, was an immense encouragement to all of us.

Over the next few days, we received many similar gifts and donations. One group brought several drums of diesel, another brought water, still another brought us food. It was never an abundance, but each gave what they were able and always we had enough. Always just enough. We did our part, searching Port-au-Prince for where supplies might be available, standing in long lines at the grocery store, and sending staff members to search for supplies in the Dominican Republic. There were even rumors of a chartered flight bringing much-needed supplies and emergency relief volunteers to GLA; however, there were mountains of paperwork and logistics required before that could happen. We were cautious about placing too much dependence on this plan, but it brought us more than a spark of hope that the future would not always be as bleak as today.

We were not as alone as we had felt that first night. Not only were people nearby helping us, but people around the world were also responding to the needs they saw on the television. The media attention that Haiti was receiving kept people's eyes on Haiti, and we received countless messages of love and support both from those dear to us and those we had never met. Besides the intangible relief of prayer and support they offered, many of them also gave financially. In spite of the difficult economic times people were facing in their own lives, the donations poured in. In fact, so many people were visiting the GLA website and making donations that we had an ongoing problem with the site crashing. If supplies were available, we now had the financial resources to buy them, whatever the price.

We were also encouraged by the people who came to help. The international community had responded en masse, and disaster relief groups and volunteers had begun flooding Haiti. Even though reinforcements had not yet arrived at GLA, knowing that people outside of Haiti cared enough to come and share our burden empowered us as well. We were not alone.

It was not only those of us in Haiti receiving this support, either; many of our adoptive families had similar support systems holding them up. While they struggled with the emotional battle of being physically distant from their endangered children, friends and family members stepped in to provide childcare for children at home, bring meals, or shop for groceries and other necessities, in addition to being a shoulder for our struggling parents to lean on. None of these things were directly related to Haiti disaster relief, yet these friends were in a unique position to provide invaluable help. The network of people supporting one another made everyone stronger, and it was a beautiful example of the body of Christ working together as it was meant to do.

We were thankful to everyone for their help and support, whatever that looked like. There was still much work to be done and a long way to go before our situation, and that of the nation, could be considered stable. With the help and support of the international community, however, we felt that we were headed in the right direction.

CHAPTER 7

CAUGHT IN THE STORM

We are hard pressed on every side, but not crushed;
persecuted, but not abandoned;
struck down, but not destroyed.

~ 2 Corinthians 4:8a–9

ANOTHER SIGNIFICANT CONCERN IN THE days following the earthquake was coordinating the evacuation of our visitors. We had four families visiting from three different countries on two continents: Canada, Luxembourg, and the Netherlands. They were in Haiti that week visiting their children and filing legal paperwork necessary for the adoption process. Although they were frightened for their children and reluctant to leave them, there was nothing they could do to help the situation by staying in Haiti. Many of them also believed that the best way they could help their children was by going home and using their firsthand experience to petition their government on Haiti's behalf. They put their trust in us to continue providing for their children while they were gone, a trust we did not take lightly.

However, getting the parents back home was easier determined than accomplished. Commercial airline service had been cancelled for the indefinite future immediately after the first earthquake. Despite the only runway miraculously being intact, the airport terminal had been badly damaged and, like nearly everywhere else in Port-au-Prince, there was no one to take charge and make order out of the chaos. Even the United Nations, who had maintained a peace-keeping presence in Haiti for years, was unable to immediately help the situation, as their own losses had been incapacitating. Once the United States' military arrived in Haiti, they took command of the airport and its flight tower. Under their direction, military and charter planes from around the world came and went, bringing supplies and evacuating survivors.

Part of the difficulty of travelling was actually the high number of flights. It seemed as if everyone wanted into or out of Haiti. News reporters looking for a story, humanitarian workers bringing relief aid, and military personnel seeking to bring order and structure filled the planes coming in. The planes leaving carried survivors, especially those who were only visiting Haiti at the time of the earthquake and who were now weary and wounded, trying to find their way to a place of safety and stability for themselves and their families. There were so many planes being sent from around the globe that it was difficult for anyone to be allotted precious time on the airport's one runway. Prior to the earthquake, around thirty planes had arrived and departed from Port-au-Prince each day. In the days following the disaster, that number was around one hundred. Many planes took off from home airports without having clearance to land in Port-au-Prince and so were rerouted to the neighboring

Dominican Republic or other nearby Caribbean islands when they were unable to land in Haiti.

Under these circumstances, it was a challenge to find the necessary flights for our families wishing to return home. Even those of us who did not wish to evacuate found it frightening to realize that we were essentially trapped in a disaster zone with no easy way out.

The Canadian family was the first to leave GLA, going to the airport Thursday night to try to catch a flight headed to North America. That flight never arrived. While they were unable to leave that night, they did meet up with Canadian representatives who took responsibility for getting them home. They went to the Canadian embassy, and a few days later finally returned to their home in Canada. Leaving their young Haitian son behind was heartbreaking for them. They begged both us and the Canadian embassy to be allowed to take him with them, but it was impossible. Their adoption was still early in the process, and they needed many more approvals from both nations' governments. Without the necessary documents, young Antony would not be able to enter Canada, and there was nothing we could do to change that. As agonizing as the decision was for them, ultimately they knew they needed to return home to their other son waiting there. We promised to care for their son in Haiti and to do everything we could to ensure that he would join them at home as quickly as possible.

As our other three families were headed to neighboring countries in Europe, we were hopeful that they could all travel together. Our Luxembourgish families found that flight, with the help of some friends back home, later that first week. It was a Belgian relief plane that would be arriving in Haiti and was willing to take them back to

Europe, but there was no way of knowing exactly when their ride would be in Haiti. After a couple of delays and postponements, the plane was scheduled to arrive sometime Saturday, January 16, and our group prepared to go down to the airport in the morning so as not to miss this opportunity. Each plane was allotted only fifteen minutes on the ground. Once it landed and unloaded, they needed to immediately board and take off, in order to clear the runway for the next flight coming in.

In addition to the parents going home, we had four children being adopted into Dutch families whom we hoped could go with them. These children's adoptions were complete and in various stages of waiting for final travel documents such as passports and visas. Under a typical time frame, they would have been joining their families in a matter of weeks. Now, however, the government and its offices were nearly nonexistent, and we didn't know when they would be functioning again. The Dutch adoption agency we worked with was efficient and helpful, advocating for the evacuation of the children. They acquired the necessary approvals and assured us there would be no difficulties from their government in bringing the children home.

Once arrangements had been made for our families and children to travel and a date was set for that flight, it was necessary to retrieve two of the children: a brother and sister who didn't live at GLA. Although we were processing Marckus and Julie's adoptions, they lived in a small home with several other children and their caretakers in Kenscoff, a small community on a nearby mountain. It was necessary for them to spend the night with us on Friday to be able to travel to the airport with the rest of the group the next morning. Because I visited every month to photograph the children, they knew me better than anyone else at GLA, and I went with our driver to collect them. For that reason, I left the illusion of safety at GLA.

It was Friday night, only three days after the earthquake, and it was the first time I had been outside our front gates since then. Kenscoff was about a forty-minute drive up the mountain road, farther away from Port-au-Prince and the catastrophic damage there. Even so, I was nervous about leaving. We were still experiencing regular aftershocks, and we didn't know if another big earthquake was coming. I was fearful of leaving the relative safety of home, concerned about what I might see, and worried that an earthquake would shake us off the winding mountain road and throw us into the deep ravine below.

None of my fears were realized, including what I saw. Going up the mountain, the damage I observed was mostly superficial: collapsed property walls, landslides on steep, uninhabited sections of the mountains, and a couple of uninhabited houses that had lost a wall. I knew that these areas had been affected, but not a lot of destruction to the houses was visible on the main road we travelled. It was nothing that could even come close to what I had seen in Laurie's pictures of Port-au-Prince. For that I was thankful.

What I did see was the evacuation of Port-au-Prince by many of the peasant people there. Walking is a common form of transportation in Haiti, and the sides of Haitian roads are often filled with people going from one place to another. On that night, though, the people were only walking in one direction—up and out of Port-au-Prince. Many of them carried a single plastic grocery bag with their belongings, or sometimes a larger bundle on their heads. This was not the normal flow of human traffic. It was a few of the masses of survivors in Port-au-Prince, anxious to get out of the city and trying to find safety and refuge somewhere else.

It was starting to get dark when we arrived in Kenscoff. After knocking on the gate and honking the horn (the Haitian form of a doorbell), a man I had never met opened the door to let me into the courtyard. Marijke, the Dutch woman in whose home these children lived, was out of the country and Alexander was watching over things while she was gone. Communication was difficult, both in actual words and in the message being communicated. Alexander was himself a Haitian-born Dutch citizen, having been adopted to the Netherlands as a baby. His primary language was Dutch, of which I knew none, and his Creole was rather limited. Fortunately, his English was decent and certainly the best of our options. More significant than the language barrier, though, was the fact that he didn't fully understand why we were there. We had been communicating with Marijke at home in the Netherlands via email, but Alexander had been unable to connect to the Internet in this rural community that he had not left since the earthquake. There had been only one brief phone conversation between him and Marijke. While he knew I was coming, he didn't realize that I would be taking the children from his care. He was reluctant to entrust them to me without specific instructions from Marijke, a communication that was impossible at that point. We tried to explain the urgency of the situation and that this was the children's only guaranteed way home. If they missed this, there might not be another opportunity for a long time. The situation was too unpredictable to even begin to guess when that might be.

Once we had convinced Alexander of the necessity of the children's departure and of Marijke's approval, he and the nanny began the process of getting seven-year-old Marckus and three-year-old Julie ready to leave. It was a long, emotional process, especially on the part of the Haitian nanny who cared for the children. She and Julie clearly had a very close relationship, and it was hard for her to let the children go. She had known they would be going home before long, but she had been unprepared for the suddenness of it and the half an hour we had seemed insufficient for her good-byes. We took a few rushed photos of all the children together with their caregivers, as it was late and past time to get back to GLA. Travelling after dark in Haiti is never a good idea, much less in these unpredictable times. Marckus, Julie, and I were quiet on the ride down the mountain. I was emotionally exhausted, but the children sat wide-eyed, looking out the windows and excited, at least for the time being, about this journey they had begun.

Once we returned to GLA, there was little that needed to be done. I checked in at the office, but everyone was just finishing the last of the day's work, and there was no more work for me that night. The children had already eaten and were dressed for bed, so I grabbed a bowl of food for my own dinner and we headed to my room, where the kids would be staying. Susan and I spread the mattresses from the first night back out on the floor and did our best to make the room as safe as possible. This task was made more difficult, however, by the fact that childproofing and earthquake proofing are rather contradictory tasks. To place things higher meant they would be in danger of falling to the ground in a particularly violent aftershock, but to place them lower to the ground meant they were easily within the children's reach. Finally, I shoved any fragile items as far under my bed as I could reach. The thought of an aftershock overnight terrified me even more than normal. I was afraid the children would wake up, scared and crying, disoriented and in an unfamiliar environment, and I would be unable to comfort them. I prayed for a still night, even more than I usually did.

Marckus and Julie seemed quite content to explore their new surroundings and play in our room until it was time to go to sleep. They exhibited the lively imagination that is typical of Haitian children who have grown up with little but their own creativity to entertain them. The few actual toys in the room—Play-Doh and a handful of stuffed animals—were more than sufficient for them. They cooked numerous meals for me out of the Play-Doh and giggled when I pretended to taste their food. They also used the pieces of an unassembled storage unit as a skateboard or as walls to their little play house. Hearing their laughter was a touch of balm to my aching soul. It was a reminder that in the midst of the hardest days of life, the innocence of children remains. If they could keep laughing, there was hope that one day I would laugh again, too, even if I couldn't see that far into the future. Marckus and Julie were a welcome distraction from the difficulties and heartbreak of the past few days.

Susan and I let them stay up late, knowing that the next day would bring many challenges for them. Adventure or no, they would be leaving everyone and everything they had ever known to travel with strangers to a home and family they had only ever seen in photographs. It would not be easy for anyone, let alone such young children. While they were having so much fun, we hated to make them stop. Eventually we turned out the lights, and they lay down to sleep.

Marckus spotted a pack of wet wipes and confiscated it to use as a pillow. The two of them whispered back and forth to one another, which we ignored as long as it didn't get too loud. By the time Susan and I turned out our bedside lamps, done with another night's email correspondence, both kids were sound asleep.

The children's good moods continued in the morning, and I awoke to find them watching me and whispering behind their hands. Their giggles were a welcome diversion from the usual stresses and cares that were my first thoughts in the recent mornings. We cleaned them up, dressing them in the clothes that had been so lovingly packed by their nanny the night before, and started to prepare for the trip ahead. In the kitchen, we retrieved their breakfast bowls of *labouwi* (a Haitian porridge) and went up to the balcony to eat. Always imaginative, inventive, and exuberant, Marckus would not eat until he had a proper table and seat. Some large foam sensory blocks we had nearby were sufficient for him, if somewhat unstable, and Julie had soon made her own table and chair to match her big brother's. The kids were easily distracted, running off to examine a toy or anything else that caught their interest, but eventually their bowls were emptied and they were given free rein to explore their new surroundings to their hearts' content.

While they played, I tried to imagine what the coming hours would bring for them and to anticipate their needs. This was an evacuation, and they would certainly be traveling light. They had their clothes and personal belongings; the only help I could think to offer was to pack a few snacks, knowing it would be a long trip through uncertain conditions.

It was still early when we gathered in the courtyard to prepare for the trip down the mountain and out of Haiti. I had Marckus and Julie with me, as ready as they could possibly be. As the time drew closer, their big adventure that had been so exciting the night before was looking more and more scary to them. I tried to focus on the positive, reminding them of what they would be gaining and trying to keep their minds off everything they were leaving behind. I had worked hard to keep their spirits up, but the unfamiliarity and the reality of their situation brought each of them close to tears more than once.

Their traveling companions gathered around them, clustered in small groups. Rutcherly had been brought down from the nursery upstairs and was in the arms of Betty, a Dutch volunteer who had spent a lot of time with her and loved her dearly. Today's good-bye was only temporary, knowing she would see Rutcherly again when she returned home, but it was emotional nonetheless. Junior had been brought down from the toddler house and stood quietly until Bas, another Dutch volunteer, and one who would also be making today's journey with the children, took him into his arms.

The two Luxembourgish couples were there, holding their sons in their arms and refusing to let them go until the very last moment. They were going home to fight for their children to join them there, but hoping these good-byes were only for a short while didn't make them any less painful. They knew exactly what they were leaving in Haiti, and they knew the dangers it meant to their children who could not travel with them. The final travelers were a Dutch couple, along with their daughter Nadine. Her adoption was not as far along as the other children evacuating, and no one was certain if she would be allowed on the plane with them or not. As her mother held Nadine tightly in her arms, the determination showing through her fear and sorrow was evident, and we all knew she would not leave Nadine behind without a fight.

The flight was not scheduled to arrive until later in the day, sometime in the afternoon or maybe the evening, but with the unpredictable airport schedules, the group wanted to be sure they were there in plenty of time. The air around us was charged with so many conflicting emotions it was hard to know which one dominated. We could not keep the heaviness of the past few days from us, in spite of our hope for today that these families, these children, would be able to go home to safety. We felt sadness at saying good-bye to the children we loved and a deeper sorrow that it had to be like this. The uncertainty and confusion were clear on all of the children's faces. They didn't understand what was happening; they could not. Yet this was the only way. We wanted better for them, but we could not protect them from the consequences and realities of our situation. We could only hope that one day they would understand the choice we were making and agree it was the right one.

Conflicting with all of those negative emotions, there was still a spirit of optimism and of hope. This was their chance, and it would tell us much about the future of the rest of the children upstairs. If this first evacuation went well, it just might be possible for some of the other children to join their families soon, as well. We would also have a clearer picture of operations at the airport, and whether we might be able to get a relief flight into Haiti.

Finally, everyone was gathered, supplies were packed, and the drivers were ready to go. The good-byes that had already been said would have to be sufficient. The seven adults and five children piled into two cars. Laurie, who was driving one of the vehicles, asked me to go along, but I didn't feel emotionally strong enough to go into town unless it was absolutely necessary. Another staff member volunteered to ride along instead, and I breathed a sigh of relief. It was yet another gruesome reminder of our situation when surgical masks were handed around to everyone inside. Their trip to the airport would take them through Port-au-Prince, and the smell of death was heavy there. The children were subdued but not overly nervous. Though the people they were traveling with were not well known to them, neither were they strangers. We waved good-bye as they pulled out of the driveway and began the journey to the rest of their lives.

The ride down to the airport was solemn and sobering, as these people saw for the first time—or were forced to face again—the realities of the earthquake's damage in Port-au-Prince. The trip was uneventful, however, with the children comfortably cuddled with the adults who would be escorting them to their new homes across the ocean. As they made their way down the mountain, the adults' determination grew, both in getting their children out of this disaster zone and in doing what they could to bring help to this suffering nation. First, however, they had to get home, and they knew there was a long journey ahead of them.

Though it had only been a few days since the visiting parents had arrived at the Port-au-Prince airport, it was now a completely different place from the one where their planes had landed. The streets around the airport were normally filled with people and activity: those who were going about their daily work, those who had business at the airport, and those who just came for the entertainment of watching all the activity of foreigners coming and going. Now those streets were quiet, nearly empty, and no one was loitering. The UN, with their camouflage uniforms and light blue caps, berets, or helmets, patrolled the area. Their presence in Haiti was nothing new, but with the collapse of Haitian infrastructure, they had taken on new roles in maintaining the law and enforcing order. Their presence was heavy at the airport, as was that of the US military.

Once the evacuees arrived at the airport, they began the long wait. They were scheduled to fly out on a Belgian relief flight, but first it had to receive clearance to land, and no one knew when that would be. The group from GLA settled in with the dozens of other travelers who had come to the airport and were now waiting on flights. As cool as it had been in the mountains at GLA, it was much warmer down in the city, closer to sea level. Since the airport building was so badly damaged, people were not allowed inside. They stayed on sidewalks closest to protective walls, finding some shelter from the tropical sun, which was hot even in January. All around them, other weary travelers sought to do the same, crowding people close together in small spaces on uncomfortable sidewalks, ledges, and streets. As the sun moved across the sky, people occasionally moved to find shelter elsewhere or to stretch their legs and explore a bit. The relief workers had set up makeshift camps, and everywhere people were on laptops, trying to find connection with the world outside of the chaos of Haiti.

Hours of waiting and wondering passed; one eye was always strained to watch the planes landing and taking off again, always alert for any sign of news. The adults were ever mindful of their situation, and they had the additional responsibility of caring for the five young children. Fortunately they had taken some snacks with them and were able to collect a few rations from relief workers at the airport when their wait dragged on longer than expected.

The sun set, darkness enveloped them, but still their plane did not arrive. As they sat on a blanket spread out on the ground, the dark night was broken only by the generator-operated lights on the buildings nearby. It was impossible to miss the similarities between this night and the one four days before when everyone was huddled outside the orphanage building, waiting for the aftershocks to calm. Eventually, after they had been sitting in the dark for hours, Bas went to the UN headquarters at the airport to ask for their assistance. He learned that the Belgian plane had not been allowed to land in Port-au-Prince, nor would it be landing in Haiti. They arranged transport for the group, as well as the others scheduled to travel on that flight, on a US Air Force plane to the Dominican Republic on the other side of the island, where the Belgian plane had been rerouted.

It was one o'clock in the morning when the weary travelers finally boarded the air force plane that would take them out of Port-au-Prince. All twelve of them were allowed to board, much to the relief and delight of Nadine's parents. The plane that had been provided was a cargo plane, ill-equipped for carrying passengers, but they were thankful for anything that would get them closer to home. There were no padded seats, no seatbelts. Instead, they sat on benches that ran along the walls of the plane and down the middle. They held onto bright red mesh nets behind them for stability, and everyone wore earplugs to block out the roaring noise of the engines. The GLA group was surrounded by other evacuees huddled under blankets and talking to one another. It was not a pleasant flight, but it was short, and soon the plane landed in Santo Domingo and the grateful passengers disembarked.

Not only was the group safely out of Haiti, not only were they well on their way home, but here in the Dominican Republic they also had access to some of the comforts they had been missing. They were able to go inside the airport, buy food, and rest in safety. Although they had not even left the island, it was as if they were already in a different world. With the exception of the disruption and activity of the relief efforts to Haiti being routed through the Dominican Republic, this country had remained untouched by the devastating earthquake and its aftermath; devastation that only a couple of hundred miles to the west was all-consuming.

The airport with its comparative luxuries was a welcome relief, yet the travelers were still not quite able to relax as they awaited news about the final leg of this long journey home. After hours of more waiting, they boarded the long-anticipated Belgian airplane. Early in the morning on Sunday, January 17, nearly a full day after they had left GLA for their homeward journey, the plane took off from the Dominican Republic, leaving the island of Hispaniola behind and taking our evacuees across the Atlantic toward Europe and home.

Fortunately, this longer flight was on a much more comfortable airplane. The children were able to lie down in empty seats and sleep, fuzzy blue airplane blankets tucked around them. Confident that the children were safe, sprawled out and sleeping as they were, the adults were also able to relax and begin to let go of the tensions of the trip to Haiti that had gone nothing like they had planned. In a few short hours, they would finally land in Belgium, and from there it was only a short drive back to their homes in Luxembourg and the Netherlands.

But some of the adults on this flight had left their children behind in Haiti, at least temporarily. Now, with their own safety rela-
tively assured, with not having to plan and stress about how they
were going to find a way home, they could not forget the children
they had left behind. Their sons were still in Haiti, still at GLA, still
in danger. They knew their decision to leave was for the best, but a
large part of their hearts remained. Their trip was almost over, but
the fight to bring their children home, the fight to help Haiti, was
about to begin in earnest.

It was early evening in Brussels when the relief plane finally
touched down. The journey had been long and everyone was weary.
The children had behaved well, but they had been through a lot, and
not only in the trip home. Their world had been completely altered by
the earthquake, their daily routine had been shattered, and they had
just spent the last day and a half travelling halfway around the world.
These kids, who up till now had rarely stepped outside their own front
gate, had ridden through earthquake-ravaged Port-au-Prince, waited
many hours outside of the airport, flown in an airplane for the first
time in their lives—in a cargo plane, no less—followed quickly by
their second flight, a transatlantic crossing. Finally, their journey was
almost over, but their new lives were just beginning.

The waiting parents of the evacuated Dutch children were gathered in a hotel meeting room, away from the hype and chaos of the
media at the airport. There were reporters and a TV crew who had
come from the Netherlands to cover the evacuees' arrival, but the
parents wanted privacy and quiet as they met their children for the
first time. They were nervous and anxious about how their children
had fared, yet excited that the long-awaited day when their children

would join their families had finally arrived! The group carried on half-hearted conversations with one another, primarily keeping their attention focused on the door, waiting for that first glimpse of their children.

Finally, the weary travelers walked or were carried through the doorway, and the children were introduced to their new parents. The family clusters spread out around the room, thankful for the opportunity to be alone in these first moments together. Now that their children were finally here, there was a tremendous sense of relief. They had been watching the news with its horrible images of damage and destruction, but now they no longer had to worry about their children's safety in such uncertain conditions.

The children were subdued, and physically and emotionally exhausted. The confusion, stress, and uncertainties of the past week were evident on their faces. They were willing to accept the hugs and comfort of their new parents, but they were also cautious, watchful, and unable to so quickly trust these strangers. While the parents knew exactly what was happening, to the children this was one more unfamiliar situation in an increasingly long string of unknowns.

While Rutcherly and Junior were alone in their new families, Marckus and Julie had each other, and the loving relationship between them was apparent. Marckus was protective of his younger sister, and Julie's trust in him was equally evident. She was by turns confused and curious about her new surroundings, but her big brother's presence gave her a sense of security. Marckus was observant of everything and everyone, as if assessing this unfamiliar environment for any potential dangers.

The parents struggled between smothering their children in their protective arms and allowing them the space they needed to adjust to their new surroundings. They gave the children warmer clothing for the cold winter weather, small toys, and plush dolls. These gifts brought a bit of excitement and sparkle to the kids' eyes, in spite of the emotional difficulties they were facing. Eventually, the parents and their children left the meeting room together. They had taken the first steps on the road to trust and to truly becoming a family.

PART II

EVACUATING THE CHILDREN

CHAPTER 8

PREPARING FOR EVACUATIONS

In his heart a man plans his course,

but the LORD determines his steps.

~ Proverbs 16:9

THE IDEA OF EVACUATION ON a larger scale, of being able to evacuate dozens of our children, first began to seem a real possibility late that first week. Until that point, we had been focusing primarily on helping the Dutch children who were escorted home by the visiting families. The day before they left, however, we began hearing rumors of another orphanage that had taken their children from Port-au-Prince to Pittsburgh. That rumor was false, but there was enough truth in it to raise our hopes that we might be able to get our children out of the uncertainties of life in post-earthquake Haiti.

As soon as the first awareness of the earthquake's devastation began to reach the outside world, even that first night, some of the parents began asking if there was a way their children could come home and out of danger. At that point we didn't fully grasp the magnitude of the disaster or, more significantly, the response and support of the international community. In the past, we had seen few exceptions or leniencies from any of the governments involved in the typical adoption process, and we didn't expect any now. As news of the disaster spread, though, and as the enormity of everything that had happened became more apparent, we began to see that governments were willing to push aside their red tape and regulations in the best interest of the children and of Haiti.

On Friday, with the first hope of evacuation, our need was great. We had received a few supplies that morning, but we were still in a dangerous position if we were unable to acquire more soon, which was a very real possibility. With this fear ever present in the back of our minds, getting the children somewhere safe was a high priority.

Some of the first evacuation schemes were a bit far-fetched, including packing up the entire orphanage and moving it to the US, where we would care for the kids until arrangements could be made for them to join their adoptive families around the world. Dixie quickly decided against that plan and determined that no child would leave Haiti to go to any country except his or her own. There would be no relocation of GLA to the US. Instead, it began to look more probable that the children would be going directly home to their new families.

I became so focused on the plans, on trying to separate fact from fiction, and on facilitating communication among the other staff members, that it took a comment from Susan to wake me up to the logical outcome if these plans succeeded. It was a very real possibility that soon, very soon, we would say good-bye forever to all these precious children we loved. The reality of the evacuation continued to change and evolve, but that one truth never did. We were about to experience a heartbreaking loss.

As an orphanage that processed adoptions, we were used to children leaving: that was always the ultimate goal. What we were not used to was the suddenness and mass exodus that we were now facing. Under normal circumstances, children were at GLA for two to three years, from the time of arrival to the time their parents came to take them home. They left alone or with a sibling or two, and we always knew when the adoption process was nearing completion. We prepared the children, the nannies, and our own emotions for their departure, and there was a transitional period of a few days, when the parents came to pick up the children before they left GLA for good. At the time of the earthquake there were about a dozen kids whom we expected to leave soon, kids we were prepared to bid a loving farewell to as they left us to take their rightful places in their "forever families."

After the group headed to Europe left GLA on Saturday morning, I began to truly understand that aspect of the world I was living in. Our children might actually all leave. We had successfully sent five children to their homes, and the governments in question seemed amenable to allowing more. The full weight of the situation hit me in a way that I had been too busy to acknowledge previously, and I felt desperate to see all of the children once more before they were gone.

It had been more than a week since I had been to the toddler house, having taken their monthly update pictures late in the previous week. Preparing for and taking the main house photos had filled my days up to the time of the earthquake, at which point our world had stopped functioning normally, and I had not had time to visit.

Once I realized that the children would likely be leaving soon, however, I knew I had to see the toddlers; I had to say my good-byes. After receiving permission to leave the office for one hour, I headed to the toddler house. It was a fifteen to twenty minute walk, steeply uphill, which taxed both my mind and body. I had time to think—probably too much time. My days had become so busy from the moment I woke up, that my only chance to be still was when I was lying in bed each night. Even then I didn't spend much time thinking, as my thoughts were troubled, and I needed my rest to face each of the endless days before me.

Walking up the mountain that day, my mind was not occupied with any urgent task, and I had more time than I wanted to think about the gravity of our current situation and my own fears. This was the first time I had been alone since the earthquake, and I worried what would happen if we had another aftershock while I was on the road. I wondered what the likelihood of that happening really was, but I stayed to the middle of the road, away from the walls and the houses that could fall on me if the earth shook as violently as I now knew it could. I walked as quickly as possible, both because of my fear and also to have as much time with the children as possible.

When I arrived at the toddler house, I was greeted by the children, and I set about enjoying them as much as possible in the time I had. Playing with the toddlers was a bittersweet experience for me. I knew it was possible, likely even, that this would be the last time I would ever see them. I wanted them to know how much I loved them, but I didn't want to frighten them by being overly emotional. The kids didn't know what was coming and, even if they had heard, many of them were too young to truly understand.

This was my good-bye, my chance to find closure, but to the toddlers it was like any of the other fun times I had visited. Thankfully, the children did not seem to sense there was anything out of the ordinary with me or my visit. I sat and watched them play, taking the time to find each familiar face, etching it into my memory. Several of the younger children clambered to sit on my lap, and I gladly held them close. Others I watched from a distance, reflecting on how each one had brought something special into my life. So often, we expect that things will always continue the way they are. We take our blessings for granted and, while we may appreciate them, we do not fully understand just how fragile they truly are. Usually, life's changes happen more gradually, so subtly that we barely notice. Sometimes, though, as on that January day, a single event causes a domino effect such that everything is different from the way it was. The ramifications of the earthquake were turning out to be painful in ways we had not immediately anticipated.

I didn't have long to spend at the toddler house, but I had enough time for what I came to do: I saw each child one more time. I had my good-bye. There was too much work for me in the office to stay away long, though, plus my attention span was extremely short. I was too anxious and restless to do any one thing for long—especially sitting still. The journey back down to the main house was as uneventful as my walk up, and I was relieved to return without incident and without feeling any aftershocks.

Later that day, we received confirmation from the Dutch adoption agency we worked with that their government was giving approval for all the adoptive children to come home. Twenty-two of our children only needed the approval of the Haitian government before they could evacuate, and we knew that was only a matter of time. We were proved right when the government issued a statement over the weekend allowing all Haitian children in the process of adoption to leave immediately. The Dutch government made plans to transport their children home, predicting the plane's arrival in Haiti as early as Monday.

As we began to plan for the imminent evacuations, there was much preparation work that needed to be done: gathering both the legal documentation and the physical supplies that the children would need. Several staff members worked long hours in the office, pulling the necessary paperwork out of files, photocopying, and assembling evacuation packets. In most cases, only the most important papers were being sent with the children. The others would be sent to the families later, once there were not so many other things requiring our attention.

My primary responsibility in preparing the files was to make sure that each child had an acceptable identification photo. We were thankful that the Dutch government didn't have strict requirements on these photos, allowing us to use any recent photograph we had of each child. We expected that the other countries would not be as lenient, however, which meant that many pictures needed to be taken, and quickly.

As the staff photographer at GLA, I took a variety of pictures, both staged and candid. Of all the photos I took, passport photos were easily my least favorite because of the strict standards the government required. Trying to get young children and infants to look directly at the camera, closed-mouthed with no teeth visible, shoulders squared and clearly showing both earlobes was a challenge, to say the least. Not only was it difficult for squirmy children to sit still, but they also had come to associate the camera, and me taking their picture, with the monthly photo-taking process when we encouraged them to smile and laugh.

Besides the difficulties of getting acceptable pictures from the children, I also disliked taking passport photos because of the challenges in getting the background and lighting right. There could be no glare, shadows, or wrinkles. Fortunately, once the set-up was correct, it did not often require adjustment.

For several mornings I took passport photos, one country at a time, beginning with the American children, who had received their government's approval for evacuation on Monday. This group of children was by far the largest, with nearly forty kids at the main house being adopted to the USA. Roughly half of this group did not have their passport photos yet. Under normal circumstances, it would take me an hour or more to photograph five or six children. Now I had four times as many, and I dreaded the task.

Fortunately, by that time, the nannies had returned to working their normal schedules, leaving our volunteers free from full-time childcare and able to help me. We set everything up, including gathering a few shirts I knew would work well for the children to wear, and the volunteers began bringing them up to the balcony to prepare for their photo shoot. I took the pictures of each child as quickly as possible, and as soon as I was done with one, the volunteers had the next one ready for me.

I know that my standards were relaxed that day. There were so many pictures to take in such a short time and so many other things needing to be done. I hoped that the governments would recognize that this was an *emergency* evacuation to get children out of a disaster zone and so would be a little more lenient in their expectations. Even recognizing that I was not being as strict as usual, the photo-taking went far better than I could have predicted. The volunteers were helpful, the kids were cooperative, and nearly all the final photographs actually met our usual guidelines. Best of all, the process took only about two hours.

Once I had all the pictures taken, there was more work to be done with them in the office. The files had to be loaded onto the computer and labeled, of course, but minor editing was also required. The photos had to be cropped to square, and I had to do some autocorrecting on the light and exposure, to counteract the bright Caribbean sun. This process didn't take long, either, and soon I had all the photos ready to go in the appropriate files.

Over the next few mornings, I repeated this process with the French and Canadian children. Even though we had not yet heard they would be evacuating, we believed it would be only a matter of time, and we wanted to be prepared. By Tuesday afternoon, the evacuation of the Luxembourgish children was finalized; they would travel on the same flight as the Dutch children. That didn't require any more picture-taking, however, as they used the same standard as the Dutch, allowing us to use a recent photograph of each child.

In spite of the circumstances and stress of taking the pictures, it was great to be around the children, spending time with them. They were our sunshine, and never more so than during those dark days.

It was such a time of struggle, of uncertainty, and kids will be kids. There is no doubt that they were often scared and confused during that time, but they were also ready to laugh and play. They didn't have the cares or concerns that were weighing on us adults, and they provided a welcome relief to us. They were also the motivation that kept us going. Seeing their simple faith and trust in us made us even more determined to protect their precious lives and souls and to do what was best for them, no matter the cost to us. For most of us, evacuating the children was not about what we wanted: evacuation meant heartache and pain. It meant saying good-bye—in many cases forever—to the children we loved and had dedicated our lives to. Evacuating these children was about doing what was best for them, both in getting them out of the uncertainty of Haiti and in getting them to their loving families.

Evacuation was also about making the best use of our resources: of getting children home to their own families so we would have the space to care for some of the many others affected by the earthquake. There was no doubt that the tragedy had created massive numbers of new orphans and children who would need our care; we experienced this any time there was a hurricane or a flood or a disaster on any level. This earthquake was beyond anything we had previously seen or imagined, and we wanted to help in the way we knew best. We wanted to provide food, love, shelter, and medical care to orphans. Evacuating our children—those who had parents ready and waiting to welcome them into their own families—would provide the space and free the resources to allow us to care for literally hundreds of those in need of temporary or long term care in the aftermath of the earthquake.

Getting the children ready for evacuation was quite a task. Many of them at the main house were too young to comprehend, but we spoke with the nannies and the older children so they would know what was coming. At the toddler house, the kids had a better understanding of what was happening and so required more conversations and mental preparation. Many of them had met their new parents when they had come to Haiti to sign papers, and they remembered the love and attention they had received from them. These children were looking forward to joining their forever families, especially since they would be travelling with so many of their friends.

Once the logistics of government approval and paperwork were out of the way, there was also the task of gathering the physical supplies the children would need for their journey home. After I had finished with the photographs, I helped a couple of other staff members collect those supplies. One of the big challenges was finding appropriate clothing for the children, as the shorts and t-shirts they usually wore were well suited to Haiti's tropical climate, but entirely inappropriate for the cold winter weather they would soon encounter in their new nations. We did not have an abundance of warm clothes, and almost all of our shoes were open sandals. We also packed blankets but, for the most part, we were ill prepared for sending children into the cold.

Not only was it a challenge to find warm outfits for the children, it was difficult to find *any* clothes for them. Of course, each child was dressed every day, but these were not clothes appropriate for international travel. Outfits that started out looking nice, quickly became stained and faded with daily wear in the nursery and many washings. This was not how we wanted to dress our children for their arrival into their new families, nor did we want GLA portrayed in this way to the media or anyone else who would see our children during their journey. Our standard of care was high, and we did not want our children to appear in any way mistreated or unloved. We especially wanted them looking nice on this, their final departure from us.

The orphanage did have nicer clothes that were set aside for special occasions such as appointments, picture-taking, birthday parties and, most exciting, when the children were meeting their parents. The problem was that only a small group of children ever wore these clothes at any one time, and we didn't have enough in the appropriate sizes for all the children to wear at once. Because our need for special clothing was so limited, we held back only a few nice items from the donated clothing we received, and the rest went directly to the nurseries. This was a system that worked well in the course of normal events, but it was a problem when we were looking at evacuating nearly 150 children, especially since we wanted to pack a spare set of clothing for each child in case of accidents or spills.

Clothes were certainly not the only thing that needed to be packed, nor were they the only issue in our packing and preparations. We needed to make sure that the kids had all the food, water, formula, and medicine they would need. We also needed plenty of supplies, such as diapers and wipes, that we would need until we handed the children over to their parents or government escorts. It was certainly a large undertaking to collect and gather everything necessary, and it took several of our staff members multiple days to make all the preparations for each evacuation.

Another struggle was the question of how much should be sent with the children. It was important that they have enough, yet we

wanted to be careful not to send too much, as we were still in a precarious position with our own supplies. We were still waiting on approval for many of the children to go home, and we needed to make
sure we could properly care for them as long as they were with us.
Obviously, the kids leaving had needs, but in a very short time they
would be in their parents' care, in the safety of a country not destroyed by natural disaster, where anything necessary for the care of
a child could be easily obtained.

In the process of doing everything that needed our attention, we
didn't forget that Tuesday was the one-week mark from the earthquake. It had been the longest week any of us had ever known. This
Tuesday, however, was nothing like the one that had preceded it. In
the afternoon, the first water truck since the earthquake arrived,
followed soon after by another! We now had access to water again,
enough to provide us with some peace of mind and to allow ourselves
the luxury of quick showers. Even more significantly, it brought the
promise that we could get more water again in the future, since the
water company had clearly resumed operations. That was one less
thing for us to worry about.

The water trucks were not the only surprise of the day. Shortly
after dinner, the Dutch consul general arrived to confirm the details of the evacuation for the Dutch—and now Luxembourgish—
children. What we didn't immediately realize was that he had also
brought with him a contingent of Dutch military—and two truckloads of supplies!

When they first arrived and began unloading their trucks, only a
few people were in the courtyard. As the commotion grew, more and
more people went outside to investigate, and they stayed to watch

the miracle of provision that was happening before their eyes. It was exactly one week since we had all been outside in that same yard, waiting for the ground to stop shaking. Now, we were gathered outside again, but instead of fear, we felt a deep gratitude.

We watched as the military passed the items, assembly-line style, from the truck to an ever-growing pile of donations. They brought milk and juice and bottled water, diapers and wipes and powder. There was baby formula and medicine, even packaged military rations. I climbed onto the hood of a car to get a clear view and take pictures, and I watched the excitement all around me. The Dutch soldiers clearly enjoyed their mission, and they were laughing and talking as they passed the supplies from man to man. I could not understand their Dutch teasing and good-natured taunts, but it was clear that their joy in giving nearly matched ours in receiving. Everywhere I looked, people were smiling and laughing, the relief of the moment lightening the stress and tension we had been facing for the past week.

It took the soldiers only half an hour to unload everything, but when they were done, we had begun to run out of room for the things they had brought us! They told us the supplies were to help provide for the Dutch children in our care. Since they had also brought the news that the plane would be arriving to evacuate those very same children the next day, they must have known those children would not benefit from their generosity. Many other children would, however, and we were grateful for it. They were the hands of God to us, whether they knew and believed it or not.

The final excitement of the night was the arrival of the relief flight that GLA had chartered. Supporters in the US had been working hard to fill the plane with the things we needed, and it had finally received clearance to land. Not only was it filled with relief supplies, but it also brought much-needed emergency volunteers who had come to help at the orphanage and lighten the load for those of us already in Haiti. These were men and women who had previously been to GLA, people who understood Haiti, and people whom we trusted to be strong in spite of the things they saw and the challenges they would face. These were people who, when they watched the news of the earthquake on TV, were watching stories of a people and a place they loved. The opportunity to physically come and serve with their hands was an answer to their prayers. They were an answer to our prayers as well.

Overall, the day had been intense, exhausting, and overwhelming, but in all the best ways. In a single day, we had gone from fear and want to having more than enough for the immediate future. Maybe we really would be okay.

CHAPTER 9

HEADED HOME

Though he brings grief, he will show compassion,

so great is his unfailing love.

~ Lamentations 3:32

WEDNESDAY, JANUARY 20, ARRIVED WITH the expectation of
the Dutch and Luxembourgish children's evacuation. It also arrived
with a startling 6.1 magnitude aftershock, which was the largest we
had yet experienced since the initial quake. Along with the inevitable
fear that the shaking ground caused, it also reminded us exactly why
we were so anxious for these children to join their families overseas.
Thanks to the supplies we had received, we would be able to provide for the children for the immediate future. Our circumstances,
however, were still as unstable as the ground we were standing on.
The earth was still shaking, and we didn't know how much more our
buildings would be able to withstand.

The nurseries had emptied after the shaking, with the nannies
once again taking the children outside into the yard. The tarps that

had arrived on the relief flight the night before were already being put to good use, with several spread out beneath the children, and one giant tarp strung over them to provide shelter from the sun and any potential rain. The bright blue of the tarp was unfamiliar, in an otherwise familiar scene. It lent both a bizarre cheeriness and a harsh reminder of the reality of our situation.

There was a lot to do that morning before the Dutch transport bus arrived to pick up the children and staff who would be traveling to the airport. Fortunately, most of the packing had been done in the preceding days, but we still had to prepare the children themselves for their departure.

With everyone outside, the first thing we did was find the children who would be leaving that day, and we then separated them from the larger group. The kids were running around and playing, happily unaware of the significance of the day. We began gathering the Dutch children a short distance away from the rest of the kids, and the Luxembourgish children in a smaller group nearby. The children were hard to keep apart from one another, though, as they didn't understand why they were not allowed to join their friends; kids from all the groups were continually trying to go where we didn't want them to.

In the days leading up to the evacuation, we had been communicating with the nannies about the regularly changing plans and the preparations that would be necessary, and making sure they knew which children would be leaving when. We had also given them the clothes the children would wear on their final farewell from GLA. Whenever possible, these were clothes that the child's adoptive family had sent him or her, but more often it was whatever nice outfit we could find in the right size. In all the bustle and confusion of the morning and the 6.1 aftershock, however, many of the children who would be evacuating were not appropriately dressed. Staff and volunteers rushed around the yard and the house, taking children to their nannies to be dressed in the right clothes or changing them ourselves, all the while trying to collect the rest of the evacuating children and keep those who were already gathered from running away.

Somewhere around this stage of the process, the new volunteers who had arrived the night before came en masse from where they had been staying at the toddler and guesthouses. At first, their appearance only added to the chaos, as new people were introduced into the busy scene. They had been shaken—literally and figuratively—by the early-morning aftershock and were now trying to grasp the realities of post-earthquake life.

Quickly, however, the new arrivals turned to the task at hand: preparing the Dutch and Luxembourgish children for their imminent departure. They took over crowd control, effectively containing the groups of evacuated children already gathered and freeing us to find the last few evacuees and move on to the next stage of preparations.

At some point, someone had the good sense to further separate the evacuating children from the others by moving them to the back yard. That provided quiet and control, and also gave the kids more freedom to move around and play without the fear of having to hunt them down again later. While the children played in relative peace surrounded by watchful volunteers, several of us staff members began the process of labeling the children.

The Dutch government had assigned each orphanage that would be evacuating children a color: ours was yellow. In preparation for this day, we had made identification tags on yellow construction paper to pin onto the children's clothes. We had also found a small stash of hospital bracelets in our medical supply room, and we put the same information on both that and the homemade tags: child's name, birth date, adoptive family's name, and a sequential number. The children going to Luxembourg also had a special note on their tags stating their differing nationality, since they would be travelling together with the Dutch children.

In addition to the labels and tags, we wrote each child's name in permanent marker on one of his arms and the adoptive family's name on the other. We didn't know exactly how the evacuation would play out, and we were not willing to allow for any possibility that our kids would be mixed up or lost. There was a lot of fear involved in sending such young children and babies on a plane with strangers, trusting them to unite our children with their families half a world away. It was frightening, but it was the only thing we could do to ensure the safety of these children and to get them out of the uncertainties of Haiti and home with their new families.

By this time, the toddler house staff had brought down the sixteen children from their house who were being evacuated. In an effort to keep their kids under control and not add to the confusion, they stayed just outside our front gate. They spread blankets on the ground and the kids had space to stretch out, talk with one another, sing, and play quiet games while they waited. Just like inside the gate with the younger children, each child was carefully identified with numerous labels and tags, although these children were old enough to know their own names and, in many cases, the name of their adoptive families.

Of course, in Haiti, things never happen on schedule, so the nine o'clock hour agreed upon as the pick-up time for our children came and went and still we waited. The departure was delayed until noon. In spite of the ever-changing information we had been receiving the past few days, we truly believed that the children would leave today, and that the evacuation would finally happen. The planning had become much more definite. This was Haiti, and we were used to things happening later than planned under the best of circumstances.

We were as ready as we could possibly be. Our supplies were packed; the kids were gathered and labeled. We waited with them: anxious, hopeful, and impatient. We had decided several days earlier who would be traveling with the kids to the airport, so we didn't even have the distraction of that decision to occupy us.

I was to be one of the escorts, and my own feelings were divided. I had thus far avoided all opportunities of going into Port-au-Prince, and I still did not want to see the destruction I knew I would be forced to face. Overpowering my fear and reluctance was my love for the children. I wanted to be with them, to be there to offer any comfort I could through the strange and possibly scary experiences of the day. I also wanted to say good-bye.

When the transport bus finally arrived in the early afternoon, it could not come all the way down into our neighborhood. So they drove some smaller vehicles up to our house, and we loaded several of our own vehicles as well. In spite of all our preparations, there was still a flurry of activity and confusion as we sorted the kids into the various cars.

One of the Dutch officials who had driven to the orphanage had a list of all our children to be evacuated, and I identified each child for him before that child was allowed to board a vehicle. He checked the names of each of the twenty-two Dutch and fourteen Luxembourgish children off his list, and I cross-referenced them with our own list of evacuees. There was so much busyness, and so many people crowded into a small space, that we wanted to make absolutely sure everyone who was supposed to be traveling made it to the airport.

A short drive brought us to the bus, which was filled with Dutch military and civilians, all eager and ready to help with our task for the day. Dutch marines provided security, and there were quite a few search and rescue personnel who were to be our escorts and helpers. We were thankful for each one of them, since we didn't have enough hands to hold all the children, even with all of our own staff and volunteers. There were many babies and small children who could not sit on their own and needed someone to hold them. Even those who could sit by themselves still needed supervision, since the oldest of our children was just five years old; the youngest was not yet three months.

Throughout the entire process leading up to this evacuation, the Dutch had been extremely accommodating and helpful, always working for the best interests of the children, and this was no exception. Our Dutch escorts were pleasant and helpful and incredibly gentle and loving with our small children. They told us that serving as our escorts was a welcome change from the sobering task of search and rescue work that they had been doing in Port-au-Prince. They were excited to be a part of something so positive—helping Haitian babies find refuge and safety with their new families back home. They smiled and laughed, tickling the children to make them laugh as well.

They worked to learn each one's name, saying they needed to get to know their newest countrymen, these future Dutch citizens.

The Dutch marines were also dedicated to their task. They were positioned strategically by the doors, their large rifles at the ready. They were there to protect us, should the need arise. We didn't feel particularly unsafe, but many of us had not yet been anywhere near Port-au-Prince, and it was nice to know they were there if we needed them. For me, sitting on that bus surrounded by fellow GLA staff and volunteers, the thirty-six Haitian children we were trying to evacuate, and our Dutch military escorts, was a surreal experience. It did not feel possible that I could actually be riding through the aftermath of one of the most destructive natural disasters in history, yet there was no question that this was real.

The trip to the airport that day was the first time I had been down the mountain since the earthquake. I had gone up to Kenscoff, but I knew that the little damage I had seen there didn't compare to what I would witness today. As scared as I was about seeing my beloved Haiti so broken, I was more concerned for the children. I didn't want any of the images they would see to scar them. Since I was sharing my seat with two four-year-olds and a two-and-a-half-year-old who sat on my lap, I was especially concerned that they might be troubled by what they saw through the window.

For the first twenty minutes, the road and sights were pretty common, but that changed when we drove into Petionville. The first noticeable change was that the park square had become a tent city. Blue tarps and blankets had been strung up everywhere, providing what little shelter they could for those who no longer had a place to call home. We also began to drive by fallen buildings and piles of rubble. At first, I tried to engage the kids in conversation, hoping to distract them from the sights outside the window. I was only partially successful, and as soon as possible they returned their attention to the windows. They pressed their faces against the glass and pointed out objects of interest to one another. As often as not they were pointing out damage from the earthquake, and I realized that they were not particularly bothered by these things. The sights didn't have the same traumatizing effect on the children as they did on us adults, who understood more clearly the reason and significance of the collapsed buildings and debris.

The damage I saw that day was exactly what I had feared. Not only was I able to observe first-hand the destruction that I had seen in pictures, but no single image could capture the scope of the disaster. In every direction, buildings were down. Houses had collapsed into themselves, and heaps of rubble littered the road. Broken walls gave a dollhouse view into damaged houses. Nowhere was the destruction absent. Even the smallest patches of open ground were filled to overflowing with the temporary structures the homeless had made for themselves, using whatever covering they could find. In some places they even camped out on the street, closing side roads to traffic.

In spite of the circumstances, for a while the trip was fun and upbeat. The kids who were old enough to understand were excited about this adventure. They did not often leave the orphanage, and they were fascinated by the people, animals, and scenery they were watching pass by. They talked about their upcoming ride on an airplane and flying off to meet their parents and living with them forever. Our Dutch friends also contributed to the spirit of excitement on the bus, remaining positive and helpful. They offered water and crackers—military rations—to the children and did everything possible to ensure their comfort. Many of our own volunteers traveling with us had arrived in Haiti only the night before, and they were excited to be involved with something so significant so quickly. We sang, in both English and Dutch, and there was a general sense of anticipation.

In spite of the excitement all around, there was also a sense of fear, of helplessness, and of uncertainty among the staff members. We didn't know how this evacuation would proceed, and nearly all of it was out of our control. What we did understand was the pain that the events of the coming hours would bring. It was important to us that the children not know our doubts and fears, especially since we knew their sensitivity to the moods and emotions of those around them. We didn't want them to pick up on our sadness, so we did our best to push our struggles deeper inside of ourselves.

As the bus ride dragged on, the kids became restless and bored, and we all became anxious to reach the airport. I don't know how long the trip took that day, but it seemed like forever. The last mile was the longest, with bumper-to-bumper traffic backed up along the airport road. While we were inching along, Dixie met up with us and boarded the bus. She had been at the US embassy, and she brought the good news that all our American children had been approved for emergency visas. This temporarily revived our spirits, knowing that another eighty of our children would be able to evacuate to safety, but the rejuvenating effect didn't last long. The kids on the bus were tired and getting cranky, and the adults were already emotionally exhausted, yet knowing there was still a long day ahead of us.

Finally, the bus arrived at the airport and drove through the various relief camps, each flying the flag of a different nation, until we reached the Dutch base. As we filed off the bus, the adults were nearly as dazed and uncertain of our surroundings as the children were. Our escorts and other military personnel at the camp directed us to a large, open tent that had been reserved for our use. We began to settle into our unfamiliar surroundings and tried to help the kids do the same.

The children had been cooped up on the bus for a long time and had been largely contained at the orphanage before that, so many of them were quite anxious to run and move about again. We allowed the kids some time to stretch and play, but it was naptime and we knew they needed their rest. It had already been a long, stressful day, and we knew it would get even more stressful in the coming hours. The older children ate peanut butter sandwiches, the babies drank their bottles, and then everyone lay down.

It was significantly hotter at the airport than it had been on our mountain, and it was especially stuffy inside the tent. We took the clothes off many of the younger children to make them more comfortable. One of the little boys, fourteen-month-old Mathieu, had a slight fever which we monitored. When he continued to maintain a temperature, we took him to the nearby medical tent.

The doctor took Mathieu's temperature and confirmed it was a little high, but nothing too concerning. The small boy was also somewhat dehydrated, so the doctor made him a bottle of electrolyte solution. Because the medical tent was positioned in such a way to catch the breeze, it was cooler than our own tent, so the doctor recommended that Mathieu stay and rest there for a while. I was asked to stay with him.

Despite the doctor being unconcerned by his condition, Mathieu had only recently recovered from the stomach virus that had plagued many of the children in the days following the earthquake and he was acting rather lethargic. I also knew Mathieu's medical history and that he had suffered from a life-threatening illness the previous year, and I knew how quickly minor illnesses could turn critical in Haitian children. I was more than willing to watch over him, especially in the relative cool and comfort of the medical tent. I gave Mathieu his bottle and was thankful when he seemed to perk up after drinking it. Mathieu soon fell asleep, and I rested as well, taking advantage of the quiet. My body was tired and wanted sleep, but my mind was too alert and I could not relax enough. I did get a couple hours of good rest, however, lying on the floor next to Mathieu's cot and eventually sharing it with him, while frequently checking his temperature to assure myself that he was going to be all right.

Fortunately, safety was not an issue, in spite of being in downtown Port-au-Prince. We were surrounded by military camps and so were well protected, which provided us with an added sense of peace. What we were most concerned about was the possibility of aftershocks and being closer to the fault line than we had been in the mountains. We soon saw that these fears were unnecessary. The military camp was set up in the middle of an open field, and the tents had no metal or even hard plastic poles holding them up. Instead, they were inflated, with supports of compressed air. This was a relief to our skittish nerves.

While I was in the medical tent with Mathieu, most of the children and other adults were sleeping peacefully. The newly arrived volunteers and Dutch workers stayed awake, comforting fussy babies and watching a few of the more active kids who refused to nap, thus allowing our exhausted staff the opportunity to rest.

When the kids woke a couple of hours later, they began to want more space to run and crawl and play. While the children had been sleeping, we had opened the tent's back flaps to allow a breeze to come through. It helped the tent feel less stifling and confining, but it no longer contained the kids, who were now wide awake and wanting to explore their new surroundings. There was a flat, open space behind the tent, and the older children were given the freedom to run and stretch their legs.

Back in the medical tent, Mathieu slept long past nap time. His temperature seemed more normal, though, and his sleeping was understandable. Occasionally, people came to visit, which was a nice break from the monotony of the lonely room. One of the most welcome visitors was Betty, especially since she had decided to evacuate to the Netherlands with the children.

Betty was one of the few volunteers at the time of the earthquake who had previously spent time in Haiti and at GLA. We had loved her before but now, with everything that had been happening, it was especially nice to have a familiar face and a friend. Betty also had taken on much of the burden of directing the volunteers, helping them find supplies, and answering many of their questions about what needed done each day. Besides being a hard worker, Betty had a great love for all the children and for us. During those challenging days, Betty was a great source of encouragement to everyone; she was quick to offer hugs and support because she understood our grief and the burden we all carried.

Betty had rejected earlier offers of evacuation, as she wanted to stay and help in our crisis. However, the stress eventually wore on her, and she knew she needed an emotional break, especially now that new volunteers had arrived. A part of her heart still resisted leaving, but she didn't know when there would be another chance to get home to the Netherlands after this evacuation. Betty also liked the idea of being able to travel with our children, and we were thankful to have a trusted friend with them on their journey. We were sorry to see her go, but we understood her decision.

When the sun began to go down and the temperature dropped, Mathieu awoke. He no longer had a temperature and was not showing any further signs of dehydration, so we returned to the main tent with the others. All of us were thankful that Mathieu seemed more like his usual self, especially as the evacuation was drawing nearer.

The hours at the airport went by in a blur of mixed emotions. I felt a battle within myself between letting go and hanging on. Part of me wanted to take advantage of each moment left with the kids, making memories and taking the opportunity to show them my love. The other part was holding back, preparing to lose these children and knowing the heartbreak that was coming. I think that many of us alternated between these conflicting emotions, withdrawing for brief times alone when we needed to regain our composure and find the strength to face the next few hours. The children sang and played games, listened to stories, and batted at the hand-shaped balloons our Dutch friends had made out of surgical gloves. We reminded the children often that they would soon be joining their families. We told them of the fun and exciting things they would experience, emphasizing most of all how much their new families loved them.

As we sensed the time drawing nearer, the atmosphere in the tent grew heavy with our sorrow, in spite of our best efforts to conceal it. We didn't want the kids to feel our grief or to know how much we were hurting. We wanted to send them off with smiles, knowing we were happy for them, and without adding to any fear they might be experiencing. So we did our best to dispel the somber mood with forced gaiety; it was all we could do.

Even if we had wanted to stop time, we could not. Soon the Dutch officials came around, telling us it was almost time for the children to board the buses that would take them to their plane. We were distressed that we could not accompany them onto the plane, but that Dutch escorts would be taking them instead. We didn't like this plan, but the evacuation wasn't under our control and there was nothing we could do about it, other than request a change. That request was denied.

We began making final preparations: checking diapers, gathering the medicines and formula we were sending, and relabeling the children. Nearly all the nametags had come off during the course of the day, and sweat had removed the permanent marker on the children's arms. We carefully rewrote their names and either duct-taped the labels back on or wrote their name directly onto their clothing.

One of the most difficult things about watching our Dutch and Luxembourgish children go was seeing them look like the refugees we refused to admit that they were. The children had been dressed so carefully in the morning, but it had been a long, hot day. A few leaky diapers had required new clothes and mismatched outfits. Not all the children had shoes that fit, and some wore only socks. The saddest part, however, was that we had to label them at all. These children had been reduced to a name and a number, and there was something dehumanizing about that. To the world, these children may have been orphans and evacuees, but to us and their families they were beloved. Each of them had not only a name, but also a story. We knew each of those names and those histories and we were heartsick with the fear that any of them might somehow be lost or neglected on this journey.

Once everyone was as ready as we could be, we formed the children into two lines, gave them hugs and kisses, told them again that we loved them, and then we led them away from the tent. The dark night closed in around us as we walked the short distance across the camp to an open area near the road, where the buses were waiting to take the children away. There we would say our final good-byes. We walked in two lines, roughly single-file, with volunteers scattered among the children to make sure everyone stayed together. I stood in the front of the lines with the other staff members so I could clearly see the face of each child as he or she waited.

For the last hour or more, knowing this moment was approaching, I had kept Farah with me. She was one of the children I was especially close to, and I needed these final moments with her, knowing that I must say good-bye soon enough. I had played with Farah and done everything in my power to make her laugh and enjoy this time together. I knew that the coming separation would be difficult not only for me, but also for her.

Now I held Farah in my arms as we stood outside in the warm Haitian night, the darkness broken by the harsh floodlights that accentuated all that was unfamiliar about the scene around us: military tents, boxes and crates of supplies, marines in camouflage fatigues, and even the tri-colored Dutch flag, waving in the slight breeze. Two or three other orphanages were also evacuating children, and they stood in similar groups to one side of us. One-by-one, the lady in charge called out the children's names. She called one of our children, then one from another orphanage, with seemingly no order to how they were grouped. The children who were called were given into the arms of Dutch volunteers who would be their escorts to the plane. They were called in groups of three or four at a time, sometimes even separating siblings. Many of our younger children were sleepy and went willingly into whichever arms would hold them, but the older children were more aware of what was going on around them and were more cautious.

The longer the process dragged on, the more nervous and tense the little faces in front of me became. Standing at the front of the line of toddler house children were two little boys. Iverson was five, the oldest child evacuating from our orphanage, and one of the few who had never met his parents. We had expected them to come within a few months to take him home. Now he was going home sooner, but to parents he had never met. Iverson was excited about finally having a family of his own but, like all of our children, he was nervous about meeting them, and especially nervous about travelling to meet them in this way.

Behind Iverson stood Djef, who was almost five years old. Unlike Iverson, Djef had met the parents he was flying to meet. They had visited in October, only three months earlier. Djef loved his parents and was anxious to begin his life with them, but like any little boy facing these circumstances, he was scared. The two boys stood facing us bravely. Every once in a while a tear would squeeze out from one of their eyes and they would look ashamed of their fear. They were young children facing burdens well beyond their years. We could not take away the fear or change the circumstances to make them any easier, but we could and did assure them that we loved them, that their parents loved them, and that everything would be okay.

Not only was it emotional for the children, but for us as well, as we watched them leave us one by one. We continued to give them the smiles we had promised ourselves they would see, but it wasn't easy. It was especially difficult when four-year-old Sarah Jean, who had spent most of her young life at the orphanage, refused to accept the hand of the Dutch volunteer who came to escort her to the evacuation plane. When he picked her up and carried her as gently as he could, Sarah Jean screamed and called out, fighting against the stronger man with all of her might.

With each difficult good-bye, I held Farah a little tighter, dreading even more the moment when her name would be called. Most of the children were gone by this point, and I knew it couldn't be much longer. Farah had grown quiet and uneasy. She sensed the tension in the atmosphere around her: the tension and sorrow we could not completely conceal, as hard as we tried. When at last Farah's name was called, I repeated again what I had been telling her all evening: "You're going to live in your parents' house. They love you and are waiting for you." With a final "I love you" and a kiss good-bye, I handed her into the arms of the Dutch volunteer. Farah clung to me, straining to stay with me, screaming when she realized that I intended to release her. My heart shattered, but she was watching me, and I was determined that neither she nor any of the other children would see me cry. I gave Farah the best smile I could manage and waved good-bye. It was a long time after she was gone before I was composed enough to turn back to the remaining children and give them the smiles and proper good-byes they deserved. My arms felt empty—emptier than they ever had before.

Soon all the children were gone, and there was nothing left for us to do but pack up and go home. It was late, but more than that, we were emotionally drained. Not long after the kids had all left us, we saw a plane fly off into the night. We waved and called good-bye to it, knowing it was possibly the plane carrying our children and choosing to believe that it was. We went back to the tent area we had occupied throughout the day and gathered up the dirty clothes and trash that had been left scattered in our haste. Now they were the only things left in the tent, and they were an eerie reminder that the children were not with us anymore.

Finally, we climbed onto the now too-empty bus and felt again the loss of our children. It was a quiet trip through the city and back up to our mountain. The streets were empty, with only the piles of rubble and debris that had spilled out into the street everywhere we looked; our driver merely swerved around them and kept going. In some ways, the damage seemed worse at night. The piles of white rubble illuminated in the vehicle's headlights stood in stark contrast to the night sky and the gaping holes where buildings had so recently stood. We also saw, and even felt, just how much debris there was when we kept swerving to miss it. When we reached our neighborhood, the bus driver let us off and we waited for our own vehicles to pick us up for the final leg of our long journey. Home and rest had never sounded so good, but we knew there was still much work to be done.

CHAPTER 10

ARRIVAL IN EINDHOVEN

The LORD your God is with you, he is mighty to save.
He will take great delight in you,
He will quiet you with his love,
He will rejoice over you with singing.

~ Zephaniah 3:17

OUR LOSS WAS BITTERSWEET, BUT for the parents, the evacuation of their children was pure joy. The days since the earthquake had been long and stressful for them. They had experienced many of the same emotions and fears as we had, but also while being separated by an ocean from the place and the children so dear to their hearts.

The families had been hard at work—petitioning politicians, public figures, adoption representatives, and the press—in an effort to get their children safely home with them. Once evacuation was approved, their work didn't lessen, but only shifted focus. For many of the families, their children were not expected to come home for at least several months, so they didn't have everything they would need to care for them. They switched from fighting for evacuation to making busy preparations for their children's arrival. They bought car seats, beds, clothes, shoes, coats, hats, and scarves. They painted bedrooms, rearranged to make space, and childproofed their houses.

The days between the earthquake on January 12 and the evacuation on January 20 were long, busy days, full of torturous fears and anxieties. Yet when the families were finally able to look back at the experience, the time seemed to have flown by.

It was a relief when the families finally heard that the evacuation of their children had been approved, but they were still anxious for the event to actually take place. They would not truly know peace until their children were in their arms. The Dutch families learned on Sunday, five days after the earthquake, that their government had approved evacuation, although they were in the same position as we were at GLA, wondering when that evacuation would actually take place, and waiting each day for news. It was a couple of days later before the Luxembourgish families received the reassurance that their children would also be coming home.

On January 21, the parents in Luxembourg woke to the news that their children's evacuation was underway. The airplane carrying their children had already left Haiti when the Red Cross, Luxembourg's adoption agency, sent out an email telling the parents that their children would arrive in the Netherlands later the same day.

It was 5:30 in the morning when the email from their adoption agency was sent out, and the parents quickly got in touch with one another, making sure everyone had the good news and reassuring each other that this was real.

One of the parents, Sonja, had just awakened to prepare for the workday when she received a phone call from one of the other parents. The news was startling and unbelievable enough on its own, but in her half-asleep state Sonja struggled to realize that this was truly happening. Her precious son would be in her arms in just a few short hours!

It was a busy day for the Luxembourgish parents, with a lot of planning, travelling, and expectation. At 8:00 a.m., the parents met together with the Minister of Family Affairs and Integration who gave them more information about their children. The plane had flown from Haiti first to the island of Curacao in the southern Caribbean, and it was now en route to Eindhoven in the Netherlands. The scheduled arrival time was 4:00 p.m., only a few short hours away!

At 11:00 that morning, the parents gathered to board the bus that had been engaged to take them to the Dutch airport. Along with the parents and the Minister of Family Affairs and Integration, a psychologist, a doctor, and two teachers travelled to meet the children and ensure that the transition would go as smoothly as possible.

When they arrived in the airport that afternoon, they found they had the privacy they would want when their children landed. No media personnel were allowed inside the room where the parents were gathered. It was a large group, as the thirteen Luxembourgish families joined the many Dutch families already waiting at the airport. About a third of them were GLA families, and the rest were there to meet the children from other orphanages in Haiti—the same kids who had waited with us at the airport and had lined up next to our children.

It was a military airport, but the Dutch officials were organized and had planned the event well. There was food available and, of course, the much-appreciated privacy. The families were comfortable during their wait—except for their natural anxiousness for the arrival of their children. They chatted with one another, listened to the regular announcements and instructions of the officials, and, most of all, watched the flight board, since they wanted the first possible notice of the children's arrival on Dutch soil. Finally, it was 4:00 p.m., and the plane landed as predicted.

It was a cold winter day in the Netherlands, well below freezing, and this was a shock to the Haitian children, who had only ever known tropical weather. The Dutch staff and escorts bundled the kids in blankets and brought them by bus to the room in the airport where their families were waiting. First, though, they underwent brief medical examinations to make sure they were healthy or, if not, that they received the medical care they required.

Half an hour after the plane landed, the first Dutch children were released from the treatment room and entered the room where the parents were waiting. The room crackled with emotion, and many of the parents started crying with joy and relief. All the stress and anxiety of the past week had led to these few moments, and now everyone in the room was filled with hushed excitement and awe, aware of all that the children had been through to get here today.

One of the first children to meet his family was three-year-old Jephté, whose family had long been waiting his arrival. Jephté had been brought to GLA in June 2008 by his teenaged mother. She was not receiving any help from her baby's father, and she was too young and didn't have the support system to help her care for the child. She recognized that Jephté had needs beyond what she would be able to provide for and she wanted a better future for her boy.

Those of us at GLA instantly fell in love with Jephté. He was eighteen months old, with a bright smile and a full head of curly hair. It was immediately apparent that Jephté had a strong reluctance to use the right side of his body, especially his hand and leg. We had our volunteers work to strengthen those muscles, and we sought help from developmental specialists who occasionally visited. We did everything we could for Jephté, but we were anxious to get him to his adoptive family so he could receive the level of care that is only available in the Western world.

One of the first blessings Jephté received during his time with us was a loving family to call his own. Far away, on the other side of the ocean, a family in the Netherlands was anxiously waiting to be matched with the child who would be the newest member of their family. Rik and Janka were a loving couple who dreamed of having children to fill their home. However, that road had turned out to be much more challenging than they had imagined. Two pregnancies turned to grief and heartache when the babies were lost to miscarriage. They were overjoyed, then, when a third pregnancy resulted in the birth of a baby boy. Stef was God's gift to them and they loved him with all their hearts. Even so, Rik and Janka knew that they had more love to share and they wanted a sibling for their son. They chose adoption as the way to fulfill that dream. When Stef turned one, they filled out the necessary paperwork to start the adoption process and became connected with GLA through their adoption agency. In October 2008, after more than a year of waiting, they were contacted by their agency with the news they had been waiting for: you have another son. They were ecstatic when they learned the news, and they eagerly looked over all the information available on their newest son. They looked at Jephté's picture again and again, memorizing his features and looking forward to the day they would bring into their home this child who had so quickly stolen their hearts. They understood Jephté's challenges and were more than willing to accept this son into their home. In their eyes, he was perfect and exactly who he was made to be—a member of their family.

Jephté's life in Haiti was not without obstacles. Many of the typical milestones were more challenging for him as he struggled with the use of his right side. We did not have a formal medical diagnosis, but it seemed that he had cerebral palsy on that side of his body, possibly the result of a stroke at birth. Jephté also had seizures, so our medical staff was always on alert and working to find the proper medications and doses to help him. In spite of these challenges, Jephté was a happy boy, one who was loved by our staff and volunteers. We celebrated each milestone and any progress he made. We prayed for Jephté's paperwork to move quickly through the adoption process so that, in addition to being with his family, he would be able to benefit from the medical advantages of living in a developed country.

Instead of moving quickly, however, Jephté's paperwork actually got held up in Haitian social services, the very first step of the adoption process. There was another child from a different orphanage with a remarkably similar name. The officials were suspicious and investigating whether there were actually two children or if two orphanages were trying to put the same child up for adoption. This was obviously a serious situation, but we had the child and his legal paperwork, and if there was something underhanded going on it was neither our fault nor especially Jephté's. We had pleaded our case and fought; now there was nothing we could do but wait for them to determine that our Jephté was who we claimed he was and then authorize his adoption. On January 12 we were still waiting.

As time continued to go by, it was hard for Rik and Janka to be so far away from their boy. They missed seeing him grow and develop during those months, and they longed to see what he could do in the environment of their home. Every month they looked forward to the written update of his activities and the new photos they would receive of Jephté, so they could see his precious face once again. It was their only lifeline into the world of their son.

In July 2009, while I was taking those pictures to send to Jephté's parents, I was privileged to witness an exciting milestone for him. While we believed that Jephté would learn to walk someday, we questioned whether he would ever do so in Haiti. We thought it might take more therapy and help than we were able to give him. That summer, however, Jephté had started showing an interest in walking. He had learned to pull himself up by holding onto the crib rails. Using primarily his left leg and holding onto those rails, Jephté could limp along the outside of the nursery. We were all proud of Jephté, and excited about his determination and what it might mean for his future development.

During the second week of July, I was taking photos for the monthly updates. Photographing Jephté was usually a simple process, because he was good-natured and smiled easily for me. This day seemed no different to me, but apparently Jephté had had enough of the photos, because he pushed himself up with his left hand and took several steps toward the edge of the table before I stopped him from falling off. The volunteers and I looked at each other in wide-eyed disbelief at what we had just seen. Jephté had walked! No one had ever seen it before, even when I asked the nannies in the nurseries. Jephté had taken his first unassisted steps. This was no one-time miracle, either. When I set Jephté safely on the ground he continued to exercise his newly acquired walking skills, going from one volunteer to another as they stood a few feet apart. Apparently Jephté just needed the proper motivation to realize he could walk. I didn't mind that getting away from my photo shoot seemed to be that motivation!

Now, Rik and Janka held Jephté, the son they had loved for so long but had never before met. All the struggles and heartache they had faced for years, and the fear and anxiety of the past week, melted away into the reality that their son was now with them, where he belonged. Jephté smiled, and they felt an unforgettable sense of rightness in that moment.

After about an hour and a half, the ninety-six Dutch children had all been united with their families and it was the Luxembourgish families' turn. Fourteen-month-old Jameson was one of the younger children evacuated on that flight. He had come to GLA at only five weeks, and we had watched him grow from a tiny infant through the various stages of babyhood and into an active, lovable little boy. Having spent most of his life with us, he knew no other, but that was about to change as he met his new mother.

Sonja was a single woman who wanted to be a mother and chose adoption as her answer. Sonja had been matched with Jameson and the adoption was proceeding on schedule, with Sonja travelling to Haiti for her required court visit the previous October. Sonja met Jameson, and they spent a wonderful few days together before she had to return home to Luxembourg and the anticipated long wait before she could bring him home. Suddenly, with the earthquake and anticipated evacuation, Sonja was facing immediate motherhood. She was excited about the prospect of having her son with her so much sooner than she had expected, but there were challenges, too. Jameson's bedroom was ready, but she didn't have clothes or any of the other necessary supplies she would need for the care of a very young child. She did the best she could to prepare for her son's unexpected arrival and, when Jameson was placed in her arms she knew that everything would be okay. She desperately loved her son, and she could learn everything else she would need to know.

Two of the last children to meet their families were brothers Ronalson and Fabien. At nearly five years old, Ronalson was the older of the two boys. He was also the more reserved of the two, but with a twinkle in his eye that exposed his fun-loving side. Faben had just celebrated his third birthday, and he was full of life and energy. The brothers had been at GLA for just over a year, and they were both easy-going and likable boys who were loved by both their peers and the adults in their world.

Their parents, Alain and Fernanda, were eager to meet their sons and begin their life together. They didn't have any children and were eager to grow their family through adoption. When Alain and Fernanda were matched with Ronalson and Fabien, they were delighted. They looked forward to the fun they would all have together and the prospect of becoming a united family. Although their adoption had been in process in Haiti for nearly a year, they had only made it to the second of many steps. They were eager for the boys to join them, but expected it to be many more months before their dreams would be realized.

Now, however, as they waited in the Eindhoven airport, they waited with great joy and anticipation until finally their sons came through the door. There was no more waiting for them; they were a family at last.

CHAPTER 11

SHORT FLIGHT, LONG WAIT

But you, O God, do see trouble and grief;
You consider it to take it in hand.
The victim commits himself to you;
You are the helper of the fatherless.

~ Psalm 10:14

THURSDAY MORNING, JANUARY 21, ARRIVED in Haiti. It was another day, another evacuation. This time, however, we were in charge of the entire proceedings, from arranging vehicles for travel and the charter plane itself to the logistics of how the more than eighty children would be cared for and who would be traveling with them. While we liked having more control over how the children would be evacuated, it was a daunting task.

We did have the advantage of having successfully survived one major evacuation, and we had learned from that experience what worked well and what didn't. When we had arrived back after the previous night's evacuation, we held a short staff meeting to discuss our observations and share how we could make the next evacuation proceed more smoothly. Those ideas were already being implemented, and we hoped that the American evacuation would benefit from those earlier experiences.

The morning of the American evacuation was full of anticipation and anxiety. There were hundreds of last-minute preparations that needed done, including gathering the supplies that had already been stockpiled, double and triple-checking the necessary travel documents, and of course preparing the children themselves. It was a monumental task and one that took all our energies to organize. In this case that was a good thing, as it left little time or attention to process what was happening or to allow our emotions to surface.

There was chaos everywhere that morning: in the office, outside, and upstairs in the nurseries. One place that was having an especially difficult time was the NICU and our nurses there. Several babies were sick and dehydrated and had to be put on IV fluids. One of our youngest children, five-and-a-half-month-old Roselaure, was the most critical. She had developed a fever the day before and was in obvious pain, but they could not determine the cause. They had given her IV antibiotics with limited success, then Thursday morning she began having seizures. As the morning wore on the seizures worsened. Even with all the nurses' care and combined experience, they were struggling to stabilize her. Roselaure was supposed to be evacuating with her brother Steevenson and the rest of the children on the flight later that day, but no one knew if she would be stable enough to join them on the airplane when the time came.

Outside in the courtyard, the supplies for the trip began piling up, and soon children, nannies and volunteers joined them. This time, only the children who were going to be evacuated were brought outside, a few at a time. At first the plan was to keep them in their nursery clothes. We had learned from the day before that nearly all would have at least one change of clothes before boarding the plane, so the idea was to change them into the nicer clothes immediately before they left. However, the nannies didn't want the kids going anywhere without being properly dressed. Soon they were sending the kids down in their travel clothes and the ones who were already downstairs were changed into something they thought was more appropriate. This process was interrupted once or twice when large aftershocks sent understandably skittish nannies running, but eventually all the evacuating children were ready and waiting.

There was a heaviness amongst most of the adults, but the kids were largely free of our concern. They were certainly used to being outside these days, and they were happy there. Some of the children were running and playing, while others sought attention from their nannies or the other adults around them. The nannies sat on the low wall around the courtyard, the same wall they had sat on the night of the earthquake, and the tension visible on their faces was not much different from that night, either. The strain of the long days since the earthquake had taken its toll, and they also knew the pain this day was to bring. They were losing more children, saying more good-byes.

The pile of suitcases and tubs of supplies continued to grow until it was longer than the truck parked next to it and nearly as wide, too. We were constantly remembering one more last-minute task, one more thing to double-check. The volunteers mostly hung around in the yard, trying to stay out of the way yet available if needed. Holding the kids who wanted attention and keeping the children calm and out of trouble was the best thing they could do at that time. I stood in the courtyard and watched it all, mentally checking off each child from the master list of evacuating children I held in my hands. Each name, each child, brought a flood of memories, and I knew this good-bye would be brutal.

Unlike nearly everyone else in the yard, I would not be making the trip down to the airport that day. Someone had to stay back at the orphanage, and that task was assigned to me. As much as I wanted to hang on to the minutes and delay the good-byes by going to the airport, a large part of me knew that this was probably best. Since I was not traveling to Miami with the children, going to the airport would only prolong the emotional exhaustion of taking advantage of each passing second and living it in full awareness of the imminent separation. Long good-byes become challenging, and I was weary enough that I wanted to move on and begin the grieving and healing process.

Five GLA staff members would be making the trip to Miami with the children. Since travel continued to be unpredictable, no one knew how long it would be before they would be able to find their way back into Haiti. We hoped that it would only be a few hours, but knew that it could be more than a week. Since most of them didn't know that they would be traveling with the children until late Wednesday night or Thursday morning, they were also busy with their own personal packing and preparations for their absence from Haiti.

In addition to the staff escorts, many of the volunteers would be traveling with the children as well. This would be an evacuation for many of our volunteers who had been in Haiti through the earthquake and immediate aftermath, and the emergency relief volunteers who had arrived only two days earlier would be helping to escort a plane full of children to their new homes. Even many of the nannies and volunteers who would not be traveling with the children were going to the airport to help with childcare until they left.

As the morning turned to afternoon, we began loading the vehicles with supplies, and after another hour or two the mini-buses arrived. They sat outside the gate in a line, ready for the children and adults to board. I stood at the gate while the line of kids paraded past with their adult escorts. I held the list of evacuating children in my hands, and I crossed off each name as that child walked by. A kiss, a touch on the head or sometimes a lingering last look were the only good-byes I had for these children. So inadequate, I knew, but there was no better expression of what was in my heart. I tried to capture the moments and memorize each little face that I knew I would miss in the days to come. Soon, everyone was loaded into the vehicles, the time for last-minute preparations was over; what was already done would have to be enough. The caravan pulled out of the driveway, one vehicle after another, and followed the winding road that would take them along the very same path that had been travelled by our Dutch and Luxembourgish children only the day before. They were beginning the journey toward the rest of their lives, leaving mine forever behind.

I watched the line of cars wind around the corner and out of sight. I shut the gate and turned to face the empty courtyard. Never in my life have I felt as alone as I did in that moment. There was an overwhelming emptiness surrounding me, and my heart was numb from the thrashing it had received. Yet there was another part of me that recognized that, as hard as the good-bye was, I was glad that it was over. The pain of the looming separation had been weighing on me, dragging on and on. My heart could not take much more. I do not know if I would have chosen to go on the evacuation flight to Miami if it had been an option. I probably would have. But I didn't have the choice, and I was, in a way, thankful when the kids were gone. One more long good-bye was over.

The only American child not in that convoy was Roselaure, who continued to battle seizures and whatever mystery illness was plaguing her. While the rest of us had been busy preparing the other children for their departure, our staff and volunteer nurses had been working with her, trying to get her well enough to travel. We knew that little Roselaure was unlikely to live long if she remained in Haiti, but could she survive the flight to Miami? Because we were unsure of the answer to that question, the nurses prepared to take Roselaure to a local hospital, hoping they would be able to stabilize her enough to fly.

As soon as everyone else was gone, Laurie drove Roselaure and her entourage of medical personnel to the hospital. The staff there agreed that she needed to leave Haiti, and they helped stabilize her enough that we believed it might be possible. Laurie had arranged medical care for Roselaure in Miami, including an ambulance to meet the evacuation flight. Now she just had to survive getting to and through the flight. Once in the USA, we knew that she would have access to the medical care that would provide the resources we didn't have, allowing the best chance for her recovery.

While Roselaure had been headed to the hospital, the rest of the children made the journey to the airport. Several mini-buses had also picked up the toddler house children, and together the vehicles formed a caravan to the airport. The trip down the mountain was much the same as the one the day before: the old familiar landmarks were gone, replaced by heaps of fallen or falling rubble. Unlike the day before, some of the windows were open and the smell of death hung in the air. Also, this evacuation included older children and teenagers. They better understood the implications of what they saw, and they were saddened to see their country so badly broken.

It was nearing late afternoon by the time the group pulled into the airport, bus after bus, and began unloading. Military tents were set up in camps all around, but there was no shelter for our group. We didn't have access to tents like the Dutch had provided the day before, so there was nowhere to wait but in an open field. There would be no shade today. The situation was far from ideal, but we had long since stopped expecting that. It was more important for the children to get home to their families than that they do so in luxury.

The group was orderly and keeping everyone together was a smoother process than could have been predicted. The children were well-behaved and sat talking amongst themselves and pointing out all the new sights surrounding them. This was exciting for them, and many sat wide-eyed, absorbing their surroundings and thankful to be sharing it with so many of their friends. The adults carried the younger children and babies off the buses and held them on the outside of the tight circle of children.

The afternoon heat was heavy, as if the sun's rays had collected in the air all day and refused to be released. January is dry season in Haiti, and the grass they sat on was sun-scorched and brittle. It was a hot and uncomfortable day.

Fortunately, there was plenty of water for the children and adults, and electrolyte solutions for the babies. Several of our youngest babies continued to be sick with fevers, diarrhea, and vomiting. Susan kept close watch over them, making sure that no one became dehydrated and keeping everyone as healthy as possible. There were diaper leaks and changes, followed by the necessary clothing changes that made everyone thankful for the thorough preparation that had gone into packing for the day.

Roselaure and her nurse escorts arrived at the airport from the hospital in plenty of time to join the rest of the children. She was still weak, still sick, and still no one knew what was wrong with her. She was receiving IV antibiotics and had been declared stable enough to travel, though, and for now that was welcome news. The nurses kept a close eye on her, keeping her in whatever shade the vehicles offered.

On the nearby tarmac, planes landed and took off, but not the one plane they most wanted to see. Still they waited. As it grew later, the sun fell lower in the sky, until the vehicles cast long shadows and began to shade the group. More time passed and the sun set entirely, darkness closing in around them.

After several more hours, Dixie heard that the plane would be landing soon, and everyone piled back into the mini-buses. During those days, cars could drive right out onto the tarmac to meet planes, and that was what they intended to do. Once the plane landed and was off the airport's lone runway, the cars drove up to meet it, minimizing the distance everyone had to walk or carry small children and supplies.

Once everyone who had come into Haiti on the plane had disembarked, GLA staff began the process of boarding with all their precious cargo. Roselaure boarded first with Cheryl, one of our relief volunteer nurses who had arrived in Haiti a few days earlier and had not planned on making this trip today. Fortunately, she had her passport with her at the airport and was ready and willing to travel when asked to help escort the fragile child. Some of the other sick children were brought on board next, and positioned to be within easy reach of the nurses. Once they were settled, the rest of the children and escorts began boarding.

One by one or a few at a time, the children were brought onto the plane; nannies lovingly carried them up the steep metal steps and into the airplane that would take them out of Haiti. The nannies had always known these children were theirs for only a time, and now they handed them into someone else's caring arms on the plane. Three staff members stood at the entrance to the airplane, crossing off each child's name as he or she came through the door. The airplane was another new experience for the children, and those old enough and awake enough looked around curiously, with excitement and anticipation in their eyes.

It took a long time for everyone to board the flight. With so many children traveling to the US, there were far fewer adults to supervise than we would have liked. Each adult was responsible for three or four children, and many of those children were dependent babies. It was now past nine o'clock at night, and it had been a long, wearying day. Fortunately, the flight was nowhere near full, and there was plenty of room for the children to stretch out and sleep. Many of them did just that, with adults scattered among them. Many of the adults held sleeping babies in their arms, while they themselves leaned back in their seats and tried to rest.

Everyone boarded, the plane's doors shut—and still they sat, waiting. Time dragged on. While they waited, one of the sick babies, eleven-month-old Marquelove, continued to deteriorate. She had been fussy and refused to eat earlier in the day, but now she was lethargic and exhibiting signs of dehydration. Dixie and Susan started an IV, and Marquelove's color quickly improved with the fluids she received. The IV was taken out, and they returned to waiting on the flight to take off. Roselaure's condition had changed little, and she was just one more reason they were anxious to start on their way. Every minute delayed was a minute longer until she could receive the medical care she so desperately needed. The other children seemed to be doing okay for now, including Atlanta, who was fragile and still recovering from the malnutrition she had suffered before coming to GLA. None of the other children seemed critical, but everyone knew the fragility of life in Haiti. They were eager to get these children home.

Finally, the plane was given clearance to take off. It was eleven o'clock, nearly two hours after the group had boarded. As the plane taxied down the runway and took off into the dark night sky, it naturally shook loudly. Those who had experienced the first earthquake (and the multitudes of aftershocks) felt unsettled by the similarity of the experience, but at least they were on their way. The kids were almost home.

CHAPTER 12

AT THE MIAMI AIRPORT

Weeping may remain for a night,
But rejoicing comes in the morning.

~ Psalm 30:5b

IT WAS NEARLY 1:00 A.M. when the plane touched down on American soil. The flight had been uneventful, but everyone was thankful to see it come to an end. They also felt an incredible sense of relief at being in the United States, knowing they had left the disaster zone that was Port-au-Prince behind them. Medical care, food, clean water, and warm clothes were no longer the luxuries they had been in Haiti, but were now an expected part of life. Our evacuees would have access to all the help and assistance they would need.

The airplane was met by an ambulance, which immediately took tiny Roselaure and Cheryl, her nurse escort, to Miami Baptist Children's Hospital. Soon, everyone else disembarked, and the group headed to their next obstacle: US Customs and Border Control. Now was when the paperwork and other elements of the children's files that had been so carefully prepared would be tested.

The group was led into a nondescript holding room with bright fluorescent lights, beige walls, and rows of airport chairs. The children and staff waited there while each child was processed. The paperwork was well organized, which helped expedite the process, but it still took a long time. Eighty children were a lot for them to get through, and the US customs agents were being thorough in their job. Each child had to be matched with his paperwork and taken to a customs agent who examined the papers, fingerprinted the child, and approved his entry into the USA. As each additional child was finished, he returned to the group waiting in the holding room to pass the time until everyone was done.

The children and staff waited wearily as hour after hour ticked by, and still the process dragged on. This was not something they had anticipated, and supplies were running low. Fortunately, their needs were met by the generosity of kindhearted airport employees and humanitarian volunteers. They provided food and formula, diapers and wipes, as well as blankets for the children to lie on. Many of these adults also joined our group and held the children, providing childcare and lightening the burden for our already over-exhausted staff. Many of the children were unable to sleep due to the bright lights and unfamiliar surroundings, but they lay down to get as much rest as possible. Some of the older children were especially anxious, understanding that soon, hopefully very soon, they would be joining their new families.

In a different part of the airport, those families had started gathering many hours earlier and were enduring their own uncomfortable night of waiting.

Expecting the children's two-hour flight to leave Haiti around 9:00 p.m., some of the families started arriving at the Miami airport a little before that to wait together. Many of the families knew one another from online adoption support groups and blogs, and they were excited to finally meet in person. They wanted to take advantage of this opportunity to spend time together face-to-face and to offer moral support to one another while awaiting the arrival of their children.

When Russ and Anita arrived to begin the wait, it was around 8:30 p.m. There were a few other couples already gathered, and everyone was introducing themselves and comparing travel stories. Russ and Anita's journey had been one of the longest: flying from Oregon was a twelve-hour trip with two layovers. Since the parents had only been given twenty-four hours' notice of the children's arrival, it had been quite the whirlwind for them. It still seemed incomprehensible that Rémy and Erlande were coming home, and that in just a few hours they would be wearing the clothes packed in the suitcases that Russ and Anita had brought.

Soon after their own arrival, Russ and Anita saw the couple they had met at GLA the previous summer, when they were all visiting their children and filing paperwork. It was a relief to see familiar, friendly faces, and the four of them went for pizza together to talk and avoid the media that was also gathering to wait for the children's arrival.

More families began to gather in Concourse G, excited and eager for their children to arrive. The group met and mingled just outside the security checkpoint where the arriving travelers passed by them on their way out of the airport. There were a few chairs, and people sat in those, but mostly people stood around in small groups or sat on the floor. They had luggage and small bags strewn around them, and they made themselves as comfortable as they could while they waited.

When Jason and Jaime arrived, they were thankful to meet up with other adoptive families they knew and considered to be friends. Samantha didn't know many of the others, but she enjoyed meeting the other GLA families, and she especially loved the camaraderie she felt among them. For all of them, it was a comfort to be surrounded by those who were experiencing the same trauma. In some ways, the families had each felt alone as they had gone through the trials of the past week. They had experienced tremendous support from their families and friends around them, but no one was going through this tragedy in the same way. They had known that the other families were out there, but now they were all together, sharing the same journey in the same space.

For adoptive mother Jill, the arrival of the other parents was a relief, and she was thankful to finally be able to relax as a single member of the group. Since the night of the earthquake, she had been hard at work: organizing, planning, and working toward this evacuation. She worked with GLA board member Tom on creating a campaign to help raise funds for Haiti and she helped disseminate information. She also created email templates for herself and others to use in petitioning their political representatives to allow the evacuation of the children. At times the evacuation had seemed nothing more than a dream, but if there was any chance of getting Chancelet and the other children home, she was going to fight for it.

As he had offered, Jill's husband, Joe, had traveled to Haiti with the emergency volunteers. Jill fully supported his decision to go and it was a comfort to her that he was there with their young son, but she missed her husband. Jill herself had not been far behind Joe in leaving home, as she had been asked to come to Miami to help prepare for the evacuation that was closer to becoming a reality every day. Jill arrived on January 19, one week after the earthquake, to offer her support and assistance to another adoptive mother whose husband had also flown into Haiti with the emergency volunteers. Together they prepared and planned out the logistics of the children's potential evacuation as best as they could.

During much of the time while she was working for GLA and the kids, Jill felt that she had, in some ways, been fighting for all the parents and their children, not just herself and Joe and Chancelet. She felt the burden of so many other lives that would be affected by the outcome of her actions, and she was determined to do her best to get things right. Jill worried that if she messed something up, everyone else would suffer for her mistake. But now, finally, the evacuation was underway. Other parents had arrived, and she could just be herself. She reveled in the company and comfort of dear friends. Jill had always known that she would gain a child through adoption, but she had never expected the friendships that had come through the journey. It was a blessing indeed.

While everyone waited, they passed the time by getting to know one another, talking, and playing cards. Occasionally group activities were announced: making a collage of all their children's pictures, taking a group photo, or eating donuts together. Though many of the families knew one another from online adoption groups, other families, especially those who had only recently started the adoption process, didn't know anyone at all. Meeting one another and getting to know other adoptive parents would normally have been an exciting event, but today it paled in comparison to why they were all gathered. Their children were coming home tonight! It was exciting, and also a little unbelievable, that they had really made it to this place.

For Jeff and Janet it was especially startling. They had spent the past week working toward bringing Rénalia home, sending all the required documents to the seemingly dozens of government offices needing them. However, it had not been until the night before, when they received the call to be in Miami within twenty-four hours, that they had realized that the evacuation could happen so quickly. It was an overwhelming prospect, but fortunately they had help. Janet called her sister-in-law, who had a daughter the same age as Rénalia and who helped her think through everything they would need. Jeff arranged for time off from work, Janet purchased airline tickets, and her sister-in-law went shopping for all the things they didn't have, and brought them to Jeff and Janet's house. They packed, slept, and in the morning Jeff and Janet's older daughter went home to stay with her aunt while they were in Florida. Jeff and Janet had arrived in Miami well within the prescribed twenty-four hours; now they waited with the rest of the adoptive parents for the children's evacuation flight to arrive from Haiti.

Every once in a while there was news of the children's progress, but the group was so large and spread out, it was impossible for everyone to hear. It was especially difficult for anyone on the outer edges of the group such as Dawn and her sister Christie, who had gone a little distance off so they could wait in chairs.

Jill considered it a blessing that she was able to receive texts from Joe, who was a part of the group traveling from Haiti. Though she didn't have the comfort of his presence, and relied on the support of friends instead, she did at least know how the evacuation was proceeding. Unfortunately, the evacuation was proceeding more slowly than anyone would have liked. Shortly before 11:00 p.m., when the families were expecting to hear that the children had landed in Miami, Jill got a text from Joe saying they were just then taking off from Port-au-Prince.

As word spread to the waiting parents, there was disappointment and frustration and, for some, panic. Anita had been hesitant to believe that this was really happening, that it could really be happening, especially while she was packing and planning for the trip to Miami. She had begun to believe a bit more as she and Russ made the journey toward their children, but now her fears were back. Her greatest fear was that Rémy and Erlande and the others would somehow be prevented from making it home, either by not being allowed to leave Haiti or not receiving permission to enter the USA.

In her moments of darkest fear, God had given her the promise of Isaiah 43:6, "I will say to the north, 'Give them up!' and to the south, 'Do not hold them back.' Bring my sons from afar and my daughters from the ends of the earth." Anita remembered that verse now, in the midst of her fear at the Miami airport, and she began to pray. She prayed for the plane and its engines to work properly, for the pilot and the US military personnel staffing the Port-au-Prince airport to get the plane on its way, and for the weather to stay clear. She also prayed that the other parents would feel the need to pray and would join her in the spiritual battle for their children.

Finally, the parents received confirmation that the plane had taken off, and they celebrated together. The children were out of Haiti and on their way home! Quickly, though, their excitement was replaced with the weight of the reality of the situation. The children were coming home! Some of the families had waited years for these children, watching them grow ever older in the pictures that were sent each month. At times, the process had seemed to drag on for so long that they wondered if their children would ever really be in their homes, a present part of their family. Other families had only recently been matched with their children and the adoption had barely begun. They had expected to be waiting a year or more before becoming parents, and while the shortened wait for their children to come home was exciting, it was also a daunting prospect to become a parent overnight.

As Jason and Jaime sat in the airport waiting, they began to feel the reality of the situation. Jean Dany and Danise were really coming home. It was what they had dreamed of for so long, but what would it look like in reality? How were the twins handling the trauma of the past week and the evacuation that was taking place while they waited? How would they feel about their new home and family?

However, the longer the waiting lasted, the more painful it became. The stress and the strain began to wear on everyone and, as the night wore on, people became less social and more introspective.

It was also frustrating that there was no steady stream of information; what the parents were hearing only added to the confusion. No one seemed to know for sure what was going on, and the information kept changing.

When the group finally learned that the children's plane had landed on American soil, complete with verification from the airport's arrivals board, there was a resurgence of excitement and energy among the parents. Their children were actually there in Miami, in the same airport. They were so very close.

It was now 1:00 a.m., and the parents knew there was still the hurdle of immigration. What they didn't know or expect, however, was how long that delay would be. It was a relief to know that the children had arrived in the country, but they were anxious for the delays and the long wait to be over.

The fatigue of the late hour and heightened emotions kicked back in. The parents waited anxiously for any information. Through the long night they waited, constantly believing that they might see the children coming toward them at any minute and so unwilling to leave and risk missing their arrival. Reports came sporadically and with partial and conflicting information. Tension was high. The parents continued to wait through what seemed the longest night of their lives.

As the night wore on, some of them lay down on the uncomfortable floor to rest, but for most the night was sleepless. Just in case anyone started to doze off, every fifteen minutes a "welcome to Miami" announcement and an update of the current time came over the PA system. The parents bought snacks, took bathroom breaks, and watched the hours go by on the clock. They lay down, pretending that perhaps they could sleep, and tried to stay warm. And still they waited on the children.

The wait was emotionally and physically exhausting. What had started as the comfort of the group began to wear on the waiting parents as they felt the strain of being around other people, especially in a high-pressure situation. At one point, the parents were told they would still have to wait a couple of hours, in case they wanted to go to their hotel rooms and rest. Dawn and Christie had a hotel outside the airport, but a family with whom they had traveled from Grand Rapids had a room at the airport hotel and invited them to join them. They were able to nap for about an hour, which was the only sleep they got that night.

Samantha went outside with her sister and her sister's boyfriend to the truck the two of them had driven to Miami. The cushioned seats were a relief to their bodies and the quiet was calming to their frazzled nerves. They were finally away from the constant airport announcements and the bustle of the crowd. They were able to wait, at least briefly, in relative comfort and peace.

As the wee hours of the morning turned to the early hours of the day, the parents were given nametags that they attached to their shirts with bright blue tape. Each nametag had the parent's name, the child's name, and the child's birth date. When Samantha and her family came back inside, she noticed that all the other parents had received these nametags. She didn't have a nametag or know where to get hers, and she worried that she had missed something important. Samantha felt a sense of relief when someone finally handed her the nametag with her and Widkelly's names on it.

It was around 8:00 a.m. when the entire group was moved to another part of the airport. They had been waiting in the same concourse since it had closed the night before, and the airport shops and kiosks were starting to open again for the next day's travelers. The group passed through the airport to a conference room in another concourse.

The journey through the airport was long and winding. The tired and disheveled group followed their guides blindly through the busy airport. They passed through long hallways, up flights of stairs, down other stairs, and around corners in what seemed an impossible maze to the sleepy, dazed, and anxious parents.

The conference room was set up with enough chairs for everyone, and there was food for the families as well. Throughout most of the night the shops and restaurants had been closed, and it had been a challenge for many of the families to find food. The stands had just started opening up before everyone was moved, and only a few of them had managed to find some breakfast. The conference room where the parents were taken was more comfortable, but still the families waited and still the news they heard was muddled.

The atmosphere was charged with the emotions of the parents and the tense night they had all spent together. There was hope, but also trepidation. The exhaustion of the mostly sleepless night, combined with the excitement of the imminent reunions with their children, made the parents giddy and nervous. Some were making jokes and taking pictures. Others tried to calm their racing emotions by writing in journals or praying. Everyone was restless. Many of them were running purely on adrenaline at this point. They continued waiting.

While they sat in the conference room, they heard a large group of people going by. They heard footsteps, muffled voices, and a baby's cry. They heard the group going into the conference room next door, and they knew their children had arrived. Their children had arrived!

Their hearts began to race. This was really happening!

CHAPTER 13

UNITED AT LAST

A father to the fatherless, a defender of widows,
Is God in his holy dwelling.
God sets the lonely in families.

~ Psalm 68:5–6a

SOON DIXIE ENTERED THE ROOM, and the parents erupted in cheers. As she recounted their experiences through the process of evacuation, the parents became increasingly thankful that their children were safely here. They also became more eager to see and touch those children. Dixie explained how the unification of the parents with their children would proceed: she would call the names of four children or sets of siblings at a time, and the parents of those children were to meet their children in the area outside the two conference rooms. In order to minimize the chaos, once the family had spent a few minutes together, they were to return to one of the two conference rooms where they could stay as long as they liked.

The children had obviously had a long night, as well, and the staff and volunteers were busy changing diapers and dressing them to meet their parents. Dixie left the parents' room to see if the children were ready, promising she would come back soon with the first set of names. Before she returned, however, the parents nearest to the wall separating their conference room from that of the children's grew still and began to quiet others around them. The voices of children singing and clapping drifted through the wall: they were singing "Sing Hallelujah to the Lord," in their native Creole. Whenever a child at the toddler house left with his forever family, the rest of the children would gather to sing a farewell to him. Now the children were all singing a final song to one another. As the parents grew silent and everyone could hear, many started crying. Some held cell phones up to the wall so family at home could hear, or to record the memory.

When the song ended, Dixie came back into the parents' room with the first four names. Samantha had breathed a sigh of relief when she had first seen Dixie enter the room. She knew that if Dixie was here, so were the kids; they were nearby, her son among them. Some of that relief faded in frustration, however, when Dixie called out the first four children's names, all of which started with the letter A. She knew she would have a long wait until Widkelly's name was called, and several other families nearby groaned as well, their children's names also starting with W.

As the parents waited, patiently and impatiently by turn, many of them reflected on the journey that had brought them to this point. Charlie and Laura's trip to the airport had been a simple four-hour drive across Florida, but their journey to bringing Wadson into their family had been much longer. They had started the paperwork for the adoption in 2007 and had been matched with Wadson as their son late in the summer of 2008. Like so many of the adoptive families, they had met their son in Haiti a few months before the earthquake. They were eager for the long wait to be over and for Wadson to be their son in their home as well as in their hearts. That wait was now reduced to the length of the alphabet.

The children in the conference room next door were also waiting with varying degrees of comprehension about what was happening and the significance of this day. Their room had only a few chairs, and most of the children sat on the floor or were held by one of the adults in the room. The children's weariness was evident by the subdued atmosphere and the fussing of over-tired children. The staff and volunteers were also weary and overwhelmed from the process of the evacuation. The younger children all seemed to need their diapers changed and there were not enough clothes for all the children. There certainly was not enough time to spend even a final few minutes with each of them; the reunions had begun.

Since the night before when Joe had arrived on the evacuation flight with the children, he and Jill had struggled with knowing they were so close, yet still an impossible distance apart. They had been on separate journeys for nearly a week, and they were anxious to be together again and to become a family with Chancelet. Now Jill waited anxiously in the room with the other parents, and Joe was with Chancelet in the room next door: Chancelet, their bright-eyed little boy with a tender and caring heart. He had lost both of his biological parents as a baby and had been at GLA since he was six months old. Jill had fallen in love with him when she first saw his picture and all over again when she met him in person. He was twenty months old now, and Jill looked forward to a lifetime of falling more in love with Chancelet. A lifetime that would start as soon as Dixie called her name!

When Dixie did call her name, Jill ran out of the conference room and into the hall. There was her son. He was in her husband's arms. She was overwhelmed by the joy of the moment, and all the pain and frustration of getting to this point melted away. Jill put her arms around Joe and Chancelet—this was the family they had dreamed of becoming; the family they had waited so long to be.

About fifteen minutes into the process, it was Jason and Jaime's turn to be united with their twins. Jean Dany and Danise had been brought to GLA two weeks after their fourth birthday. When they arrived at GLA, Jean Dany's easy-going nature had helped him quickly adapt to the routine at GLA, but there was often a longing look in his eye, an eagerness to fully belong. Danise found the transition to orphanage life more difficult than her brother. Danise had an inner strength, however, and a strong sense of self that served her well. Both children longed for the love of a family, and we looked forward to the day when each of them would receive the individual love and attention they deserved. Now that day was here, and six-year-olds Jean Dany and Danise were as eager to meet their parents as Jason and Jaime were to meet them.

When Jason and Jaime stepped out into the hall, Jean Dany flung himself toward them and greeted them both with a big hug. Danise was fighting illness as well as the journey's fatigue, so her greeting was more subdued, but she was also happy to be with her parents at last.

Russ and Anita had felt called to adoption as a way of living out their love for Christ. God has a special place in His heart for the vulnerable, especially orphans and widows, and He asks His followers to love and care for them as well. For Russ and Anita that meant completing their family through adoption. As they watched couples leave the room to become parents, whether for the first time or all over again, they understood more clearly than ever the joy that our heavenly Father feels in adopting us into His eternal family.

The hall was crowded with people when Russ and Anita were called out of the conference room, but their attention focused in on the two people they most wanted to see at that moment: their son Rémy and daughter Erlande. They looked so much smaller in the busy hallway, but they were here. Rémy looked excited and nervous, and recognition flashed across his eyes when he saw the parents he had met the previous summer. Erlande looked scared and tired. Anita ran to them and dropped on her knees in front of them, wrapping them both in a big hug. Russ was not far behind Anita, and they shared in the relief and joy of having their children with them here and now. They held their children close and told them how much they loved them. When they had left Haiti the previous summer, Russ and Anita had promised Rémy they would come back for him and Erlande, and this moment was the completion of that promise.

Rémy had arrived at GLA when he was six years old, a loving and affectionate boy. As he had grown older, he spent more time with the bigger boys playing basketball or riding around on scooters rather than seeking attention from the nannies and volunteers. One thing that never changed, though, was his devotion to Erlande. He was a protective big brother who watched out for his little sister. Even though Erlande was not quite two years old when she came to GLA, she had lived at the toddler house instead of the nurseries because that was where Rémy was. As the youngest child by far, and a girl at that, Erlande was everyone's darling, pampered and petted. The older girls especially loved to dress her up and carry her around, and Erlande loved the attention she received. Rémy was now only a few weeks away from his eighth birthday and Erlande was three. They had left GLA behind and had joined their new family. They were together, as they had always been throughout life.

After a few minutes, Russ, Anita, Rémy, and Erlande moved into the conference room where their children had so recently been waiting and where other children still waited for their turn to meet their parents. As time went on, the ratio shifted as children were replaced by families. Russ and Anita delighted in the deceptively simple pleasure of playing with their children as they sat next to their friends and the daughter they had just been united with, as well. They knew the truth that the families being brought together today were a miracle from the hand of God.

In the parents' room, Dawn waited nervously for Naïka's name to be called. Would she recognize her daughter, or had she grown too much since the previous August when she had first met Naïka in Haiti? Was she really ready to be a mom? Dawn had been working toward this adoption for so long, and had known Naïka as her daughter for more than a year, that she had believed herself to be emotionally and mentally prepared for a long time. However, as Naïka's homecoming became more of an imminent reality, she had realized all the things that still needed to be done: Naïka's crib taken out of the box and set up, electrical outlets covered and the house childproofed, clothes and shoes bought for Naïka. By the time she had left for Miami, Dawn and her sister had completed those tasks, and Dawn felt better about her preparedness for Naïka's arrival. Now, as she waited for Naïka's name to be called, some of those concerns resurfaced.

Dawn's daughter, twenty-one-month-old Naïka, had come to GLA at only four weeks old. The bustle and busyness of the orphanage was the only home she had ever known. She had left that home yesterday, and soon she would be joining her mother and moving to Michigan. Naïka had obviously grown and changed quite a bit in her time with us, from a tiny baby to an increasingly energetic toddler. When she had been a little younger, Naïka had loved to stand in her crib, absorbed in the antics of the children and taking in everything that was happening around her. As she grew older, she was transitioning from merely watching the other children to joining them in their play. Her confidence and personality were revealing themselves more all the time. Now, however, Naïka was exhausted from the long trip and sleepless night. Soon she would have a chance to sleep, but what was even more important was that she would receive the gift of a loving mother.

Somewhere in the middle of the reunions, Naïka's name was called and Dawn eagerly went to meet her daughter. The meeting area was crowded, and it took Dawn a few moments to find Naïka, but there she was in a volunteer's arms. Dawn knew and recognized her daughter, even without the duct tape nametag on the back of the pink and white flowered dress that Dawn and her sister had taken to Naïka the previous summer. All of Dawn's doubts faded away. She reveled in the feeling of holding her daughter and knowing that this time it was forever.

Rénalia had come to GLA through a disaster—flooding that had devastated the rural town where she had been born—and now it was a disaster that was bringing her home to her forever family. Rénalia had been sixteen months old when she came to GLA a little over a year before and, like many children, she had been quiet and withdrawn when she first arrived. As she began to adjust to the orphanage and trust our staff and volunteers, though, Rénalia began to show us her sweet and loving heart. Rénalia was one of the children who had especially enjoyed all the time spent outside since the earthquake. She was an energetic two-and-a-half-year-old who loved exploring her surroundings. We loved her excitement and her bright smile.

Although not at the very end, Rénalia's name was low on the list. By the time her name was called, Jeff and Janet were more than ready to be reunited with the daughter they knew through pictures and a brief visit the previous fall. They held their daughter with joy in their hearts. Rénalia was in their arms and would soon be in their home, no longer separated from them by hundreds of miles and international borders. She was where she belonged: a part of their family.

While Charlie and Laura and their daughter Naomi waited their turn to meet Wadson, they loved watching the other family reunions that were taking place. Each time another child's name was called and his or her parents rose to meet their child, everyone clapped and cheered. Beyond the excitement of their own reunions, there was a sense of camaraderie among the group. Each family had traveled their own road to this moment, but right here, right now, they shared this excitement. They knew the pain of the past ten days, and now they were united in the joy of this reunion. It was an experience they shared with one another alone and that no one outside that room would ever truly be able to understand.

Charlie and Laura's son, Wadson, had just passed his third birthday, but he had been at GLA since he was fourteen months old. Wadson's smile and affectionate personality had always won over anyone who met him and, as he grew, his playful nature became more apparent, as well. He was an active little boy with a mischievous twinkle in his eyes that showed his love for life and fun. Although small for his age, for several months Wadson had been one of the biggest boys in the nurseries, and only a few weeks earlier he had been moved to the toddler house. There had been a lot of disruption to Wadson's life and routine recently, but that was about to change since this transition was permanent.

By the time Wadson's name was finally called, most of the other family reunions had already taken place. Charlie and Laura had been waiting for this moment for what seemed like forever, and they were excited to finally see him and have their family together and complete. It was their turn at last, and they walked out into the hall where Wadson was waiting for them, his own family. The wait had been long, but now that Wadson was in their arms, they knew that every minute had been worth it.

Life had been more than a little chaotic for Samantha since she had first learned of the earthquake, ten days earlier. As soon as she saw the extent of the damage to the Haitian government in Port-au-Prince—the death of key adoption officials and the complete destruction of several court buildings—she had recognized that the evacuation of Widkelly was a possibility because of the extreme circumstances. Having been matched with eighteen-month-old Widkelly only two months earlier, Samantha knew she had a lot of preparation to do if there was any chance her son would be coming home. Up to that point, the earliest she had let herself hope to have her son home was by Thanksgiving the following November, but she knew that his actual homecoming would likely be more than a year away.

Samantha started the preparations for Widkelly's possible sooner-than-expected arrival by informing her boss at work. Since she was still so early in the process, Samantha had not yet told anyone there that she was adopting. She told them now, explaining that, because of the earthquake, Widkelly might possibly be coming home soon, and she began the process of transitioning her work to her colleagues. Since Samantha's sister was planning to come help out during Widkelly's first month home, her sister also began the process of getting the necessary time off work to be ready whenever Samantha needed her.

Samantha started thinking about what supplies she would need to care for a young child, since she currently had nothing ready. The room that was to be Widkelly's had no bed, and the dresser was full of Samantha's things. Only the previous Sunday she had learned that her son would be eligible for a humanitarian parole visa, and she knew that she had only days until he came home, not the weeks or months that she had previously thought the evacuation would take. Anything she needed to do before Widkelly came home needed to be done immediately.

On Wednesday, Samantha was still awaiting final word on the children's travel plans and where she would need to be and when, when she went shopping with a friend for a car seat. Wherever she ended up meeting Widkelly, Samantha knew she would need a car seat to get him home. While shopping, Samantha also realized her son would need diapers, since he was much younger than she had anticipated he would be when he arrived home. Fortunately, another shopper in the store had children the same age as Widkelly and offered helpful advice about which diapers to buy and where to get them for a good price. Samantha also purchased the necessary toiletry items and baby food, as well as groceries for herself and her sister, since the cupboards at home were nearly bare.

Throughout her shopping trip, Samantha had continually been checking her phone for any word about the children's travel plans. Finally, at 8:00 p.m. she saw the email she had been waiting for. The kids' evacuation flight would be arriving in Miami the next evening. With twenty-four hours until she needed to be in Miami, Samantha bought her plane ticket, thankful that from Chicago to Miami was an easy non-stop flight that ran several times a day. Samantha's friend helped her childproof the house and pack. By noon the next day, Samantha was on her way to Miami and Widkelly.

The wait at the airport had been Samantha's own particular version of labor, and she was ready for the eternal waiting to be over. An hour after Dixie had first entered the conference room, she at last called Widkelly's name. Samantha hurried out of the conference room and into the meeting area, but her son was not there. Where was he? Where was Widkelly? The meeting area was crowded and chaotic with united families and GLA staff and volunteers and news crews with cameras, but no Widkelly. Samantha asked a man with a "Just Ask Me" button on his shirt where her son was, and he went into the children's room to find out. Half a minute that felt like an eternity later, Widkelly was brought to the door, a bottle of chocolate milk in his hands. Samantha recognized small changes in her son from the photographs she had memorized—the scar on his forehead had faded and he had gotten more teeth—but this was the same adorable boy with the eyes she had fallen in love with. He was hers, now and forever.

Widkelly had been one of the newer children at GLA, having been with us for only a few months. He was a sweet-natured and happy boy whom we were thankful to see join his mother so quickly. Samantha and Widkelly could now be mother and son together, rather than Widkelly growing every month a little older with Samantha watching from afar.

Soon there were no more evacuated children, only united families.

CHAPTER 14

AN OCEAN APART

He gives strength to the weary
And increases the power of the weak.

~ Isaiah 40:29

IT WAS NOT UNTIL I arrived in the office on Friday morning that I learned the American children had been stuck in immigration all night and were only then meeting their families. It had been a long night, no doubt, but joyful reunions were taking place that very minute. I longed to be a part of those reunions, to feel some of the joy of the children's evacuation, rather than only the pain and loss that was my own share in the experience.

The emptiness at GLA was tangible, and I had been suffocating on it since everyone had left the day before. The nannies and I felt grief and the absence of the many children who had so recently been with us, in our arms. We didn't begrudge them their families, but still our hearts ached. That sorrow only added to the pain of the trauma we had not chosen to live. In less than twenty-four hours' time, we had said good-bye to 120 children. Only thirty-six were left, and we had every expectation that they would soon be leaving as well.

Saying good-bye to so many at once certainly took its toll, but there were other factors that had combined to make the recent evacuations climactic. Those kids left Haiti within nine days of the earthquake, but we had lived lifetimes during those days. We had been going non-stop, and the emotional toll was catching up to our bodies.

The days between the earthquake and the evacuations were roller coasters of up and down, of good news and devastation. Even the evacuations themselves were uncertain, and we never knew from one day to the next what would be happening, how they would take place, or if there was some new obstacle to overcome. We lived in extremes, from not knowing if we would have the supplies we needed for the days ahead to having more than enough to share with others. We were emotionally exhausted.

Even in Miami, there was pain in the family reunions for several of our staff members. The physical exhaustion from the journey and the long night helped numb their emotions and the feelings of loss as they bid a final, in many cases a forever, good-bye to the children. Sooner than they had imagined possible, the families had united and gone off to start their lives together. The staff members were suddenly alone in the empty conference room that had so recently been full of life and excitement, eagerness, anxiety, and the whole range of human emotions. Now they stared blankly at one another, trying to understand how it could all be over so soon. They had expected at least one or two of the children's parents to have been delayed, and they had anticipated caring for them during that wait. Once they had gotten through the eternal delays and red tape of customs, however, the reunions had happened so much quicker than anyone had believed possible. With the evacuation complete, responsibility and adrenaline no longer seeped from their pores, and they felt the same emptiness I had experienced the day before as I watched them drive away from the courtyard.

They left the conference room, with its bittersweet memories of heartbreaking good-byes and loving parents, and headed to their hotel rooms. Their mission of escorting the children to their American families had been accomplished, and now they were stranded in Miami, eager to return to Haiti and the orphanage that needed them. They had a chartered plane available, but it was entirely at the mercy of the Port-au-Prince airport operators regulating the hundreds of flights wanting to land each day. No one knew if it would be a few hours, days, or even weeks before they would be able to make their way back.

Back in Haiti, in spite of the unnatural quiet and inordinate stillness of an orphanage that was usually bursting with life, there were still children in our care: children needing to go home. Early Friday morning I went to the toddler house to take identification photos of the few remaining children who didn't yet have one.

The courtyard I entered was the same one where I had visited with the children hundreds of times, but the pervading emptiness could be felt there, too. Only thirteen of our children were left at the toddler house, along with three children of staff members who no longer had homes. The kids seemed a little lost, unsure of what to do now that the life they had known had fallen apart. These children were older than the ones at the main house, and they better understood what was happening in the world around them. The earth had shaken, was still shaking, and no one knew what was going to happen next. Their friends had left, and these children too felt the pain of that loss. They had been told they would also be going to live with their families, but they didn't know when. No one knew when.

I appreciated the opportunity to spend time with the kids, to see their familiar faces and brave smiles, and to give the hugs that were the only true comfort I could offer. I didn't have the answers to all the questions they asked, but I offered them my love and as much reassurance as I could honestly give. Unfortunately, because of the urgency of getting the pictures taken and processed, I had only a few minutes to spend with them. If they were to go home, I needed to get the pictures taken and sent off for their government's approval.

It took me a few minutes to find acceptable clothes and a location to take the photos, but since time was limited, I did the best I could with what I could find. While three-year-old Saraphina stood in the doorway watching me dig through boxes to find an acceptable shirt for her, I felt the earth tremble and I heard the windows rattle. I ran to Saraphina and put my arm around her, shielding her as best I could and trying to calm her fears. The look she gave me was more confusion than fear, however, as though she had absolutely no idea what was going on in her world. Things had become very strange, and she didn't know what to make of it all.

Soon I had finished taking the pictures I had come for, and I hurried back to the main house to get the pictures processed and sent with the children's files. As is usual in situations requiring urgency, the computer and printer were not cooperating. Eventually, however, Laurie and I got everything working, and the pictures were cropped, printed, cut, labeled, and matched with the appropriate files. A staff member took them to the Canadian embassy that morning, and we were optimistic that the children would be approved to join their adoptive families.

Once the rush of work required for preparing those files was over, there was enough calm that I thought I would try visiting the nurseries. I hadn't been upstairs to see the children since the Americans had left the day before. I knew that the twenty-two children still there would not come close to filling the nurseries, and I had not felt prepared to face the absences. The children who remained at GLA were dear to me, but on the day of the evacuation I felt the loss of the others too deeply. I was only too aware that I would very likely be saying good-bye to these children soon, and their little faces would only remind me of that fact. There had already been too much sorrow and too much sadness with the exodus of the American children.

Today, however, I was ready to see them again, to hold them and feel their little arms around my neck. I also knew I needed to face the nearly empty nurseries, to see what it was like with so many of our children gone. When I went upstairs, I was surprised when only silence greeted me. I walked through the nurseries and saw no one—not a child, not a nanny. I checked the upstairs balcony, but they weren't there, either. I could catch the sound of children's voices, but could not figure out where they were coming from, since the children were clearly not inside, and I had not seen them outside, either. Eventually I did find them outside, but in the back of the house, rather than in the front where they had usually been staying. No doubt the morning's aftershock had driven them outside yet again, and the fewer children made the smaller space in back an appealing option.

Seeing so few kids remaining was a shock, but the individual children were a comfort to me. Their resilience and ability to laugh and play made everything worthwhile, and made me more committed to helping them get home to safety and their families. In spite of their reduced number, when they were excited it sounded as though there were just as many children as there had always been.

Later that day, I had the opportunity to go back to the toddler house when some television reporters came for a story and wanted video of the older kids. I went with them, thankful for the chance to visit the kids again and spend more time with them. It was naptime, but the kids and nannies were all outside. The children were laying down under and on top of the play equipment, boys on one side of the courtyard and girls on the other. Some of the kids were already asleep, but others were awake and more than willing to skip naptime in favor of playing in front of the camera.

I spent my time with one of the little girls, tickling her and holding her upside down. Rachelle was nearly three years old now, though I remembered her as the infant she had been when I arrived two years before. Current events had made me reflective about each of these children and how they had changed and grown during my time with them. Rachelle was a beautiful girl, but it was her smile and her joy that made her special. As we played together, I prayed that she and her brother and all the rest of these children would soon be able to go home.

We continued to have visitors at the orphanage who needed our time and attention: media personnel, reporters, journalists, and cameramen from around the world. They asked questions, conducted interviews, and wanted tours of the facilities. Humanitarian workers from various social service organizations, both Haitian and international, also came. They asked questions and wanted to know the state of our buildings and current circumstances. How many children did we have? Were they safe? Did we have enough supplies to provide for them? Some offered assistance, but most just asked their questions and left.

The GLA contingent in Miami was also hard at work. After they rested from the exhaustion of their trip and the emotions of the past week and a half, they started doing what they could while they waited on a return flight to Haiti. They were no longer in a country that had been crippled by a massive earthquake. They were no longer in a country that daily struggled to get by even before the devastation. There were stores everywhere, with shelves full of the supplies we were so desperate for in Haiti, so they went shopping. Since the plane (whenever it would be allowed to return) was a chartered flight, there would be no baggage restrictions, so the group loaded up.

They went to large grocery stores and mega-marts, buying food and supplies for the orphanage: rice, beans, sugar, oil—everything in the largest quantities they could find. They also bought relief supplies for the orphanage staff, many of whom had lost their homes. They bought lanterns and flashlights and tarps and bottled water and blankets, leaving one store with empty shelves and not a single blanket left. They also bought large plastic storage bins and tubs for transport and for use in Haiti. When they returned to the hotel, they packed the tubs and prepared them for their trip home. It was heavy work, with many of the bulk food items in fifty-pound bags.

Yet when the shopping was done and the packing finished, they still had nowhere to go. They were still stuck in Miami. They had meetings to discuss their situation and how to get back to Haiti most quickly. Though some were in favor of flying into the Dominican Republic and taking a bus back to Haiti, the final decision was to stay in Miami and wait for their flight to be approved to travel to Port-au-Prince.

The waiting and forced inactivity began to reveal the depth of trauma they had experienced in the earthquake and the following days. Even in Miami they felt the ground shaking. Of course there was no earthquake there, and no aftershocks—it was only their minds playing tricks on them. They felt the fear that was never absent in those days; the fear that something terrible was only a breath away. In Haiti that danger was real and natural, but when the fear followed them to Miami, they began to realize they were suffering from a deeper trauma than they had realized.

Eventually they learned that their flight would be able to return to Haiti on Monday, four days after they had left Haiti with a plane full of American children. They still had more waiting and too much time to think, but at least there was an end in sight.

While they were waiting in Miami, we did have the opportunity to evacuate two of our French children. Late on Friday afternoon, a representative from the French embassy had shown up at GLA with a scrap of paper listing children approved to evacuate. One of the names on that paper was Daniel, a little boy from the main house who had turned two several months earlier. We were told to take him to a French school in Petionville the following morning. The French embassy would be conducting the evacuation, and we were simply to show up. We confirmed with Dixie that Daniel could leave, though we knew that any children leaving would be on the French government's terms, not ours.

I packed a bag for Daniel, trying to imagine what supplies he would need for the long trip and not knowing what would be provided for him. I packed the same things we had been sending with the other evacuees—clothes and snacks and water and diapers—but fortunately in a much smaller quantity, since it was only one child.

Early Saturday morning, I got myself and Daniel ready for the trip down the mountain. Just as we were getting ready to leave, the French called to tell us the departure time had been delayed by a few hours. We also received approval for another child to go, Josef, who was almost three years old. Now I would be taking both boys to the French embassy's meeting point, and I had more packing to do.

When we left that morning, our first stop was at the toddler house to pick up Josef. We had not been able to communicate with them, so no one there knew that we were coming or that Josef was leaving with us. Once they understood the situation, however, they were quick and efficient and had Josef and his things ready in just a few minutes. We also asked Josef's nanny to come along, and soon she and Josef joined Daniel and me and we began the trip down the mountain to Petionville.

I had previously left GLA to go up to Kenscoff and, more recently, I had been a part of taking the Dutch and Luxembourgish kids to the airport earlier in the week. I had certainly seen the damage the earthquake had done, but even so, this trip showed me fresh examples of the earthquake's devastation. The areas where we were traveling were more residential, more affluent. In one such area, nearly every house had at least partially fallen and some were completely flattened. There were people working to remove the debris and clean up, not with the urgency of searching for anyone under the rubble, but simply trying to move on with their lives and clean up the wreckage of the past. Even the fact that we could drive down this road at all, as tight as it was in places, was a testament to how much debris had already been removed, because it was obvious the road had been completely blocked at one time.

The boys did well throughout the trip, not fussing or crying, even though they knew something strange was happening and they didn't fully understand what. Daniel clung to me a little tighter than normal, but he was happy to eat the military-ration crackers I had brought, drink water, and look out the windows as we rode along. Josef was similarly occupied and content with his nanny in the seat behind us.

When we arrived at the school's gate, we were greeted by armed guards, which is typical in Haiti. They directed us toward our meeting point, which was a building not far from the entrance. In the opposite direction was a makeshift hospital that had been set up, and I was thankful that was not the reason we had come. We found the building we were looking for, and I entered the classroom where the representative from the French embassy was waiting. Josef stayed outside with his nanny, but Daniel came in with me. It was a fairly typical elementary school classroom with toys and big alphabet letters, and Daniel played while I provided the embassy representative with the information she needed.

I had been prepared with most of the necessary information, things like the children's names and birth dates and adoptive family names. The embassy representative did ask a few questions that I didn't have the answers to, so I had to call back to the orphanage to get that information. Fortunately, we were able to get everything she needed, and the lady told me I was free to leave. The children would stay at the school, and in a few hours they would be taken to the French embassy. From there they would board the planes that would take them to their waiting families in France. The children were now in French custody; there was no reason for me to stay any longer.

Josef's nanny agreed to stay with the boys until they left, and the French representative offered to bring her home after they had gone. She was familiar and so a comfort to Josef, who stayed close to her side, but Daniel didn't know her and was upset to see me leave.

Daniel was normally an active, rambunctious little boy who was full of life and personality, but today he was quiet and nervous and clingy. It was a drastic change from a child who was one of the oldest at the main house and who was, in many ways, king of the nursery. It was hard to see him so scared, and I felt helpless knowing there was nothing I could do to change that. His crying and screaming tore at my heart as I was forced to walk away. It was the second time in less than a week that I had experienced such a traumatic good-bye.

My only comfort in walking away from Daniel, in seeing and hearing his pain, was the belief that what I was doing was for the best. We had started receiving pictures from the families of the children who had already arrived home. Though the children had obviously been through a difficult time, you could see the love in their families' eyes. Some of the children were even smiling, and you could see that they were beginning to learn to love and trust these new families. I knew that Daniel had a better future elsewhere, even if there was no way his mind could comprehend it.

It was a long, quiet ride back up the mountain, made even longer because the UN was working on the road, clearing away fallen debris to make the roads safer and wider. It probably wasn't as long as it felt, but the tumultuous emotions and painful memories made it feel interminable. I could not even numb my thoughts by meaningless busywork, but was forced to sit quietly and think.

Finally, we made it back to GLA and the never-ending work of trying to evacuate more children, answering phone calls and emails, and dealing with the various visitors who continued to come. Although we were still busy, in many ways we were in the calm after the storm. The frantic packing and planning for the evacuations was over. We knew any major decisions could wait until Dixie came back from Miami, and we eagerly anticipated the return of the staff. Those were challenging days for all of us, but God was faithful and gave us the strength we needed to keep going. The children were also a tangible encouragement whenever I became overwhelmed or stressed. They were often the spark of love and joy and motivation I needed to keep going. It was always bittersweet, however, because they were also a reminder of the next loss, the next good-bye I would face.

CHAPTER 15

CONFUSION AND UNCERTAINTY

You hear, O LORD, the desire of the afflicted;
You encourage them, and you listen to their cry,
Defending the fatherless and the oppressed.

~ Psalm 10:17–18a

WITHIN A WEEK OF THE earthquake, the only countries that had not approved emergency evacuation of their adopted children were France and Canada. This was especially surprising from the Canadian government, since they were usually one of the quickest and most efficient when it came time for us to request visas for the children. In this case, however, the entire process seemed slow and frustrating, both for GLA staff and the adoptive families waiting at home.

Although not directly connected to the delay, Canadian adoptions were primarily independent, meaning that we communicated directly with the families, rather than through an adoption agency. The families from the Netherlands and Luxembourg were required to adopt through an agency, and we worked with one agency in each nation. Similarly, almost all of our American adoptions were processed through a single agency that helped funnel communication between GLA and the families. Because we didn't have any such liaison to help expedite communication with the Canadian families, a former staff member offered to step into that role. Léa and her husband had previously worked in GLA's office in Haiti and, besides understanding how Haitian adoptions worked and knowing many of the adoptive families, Léa was in law school, studying immigration law. It was a perfect fit.

Besides communicating the facts and latest updates to the families, Léa gave them positive ways to help their children. Like the parents in the other countries, they contacted their local, provincial, and national representatives, fighting on behalf of their children. Some of the delay seemed to be caused by a confusion as to how to deal with these children. Victims of natural disaster didn't qualify for refugee status, and there was no precedent for allowing children with incomplete adoption paperwork into Canada. There also seemed to be a sense of general confusion. Different families were hearing different stories from their government officials, and some officials were denying that other nations had allowed evacuation for any of the children, even after GLA kids had already landed on European soil. In the midst of all this confusion, the families shared their stories with Léa and one another and did their best to sort out the truth.

Besides contacting their political representatives, the families also used the news media's attention to try to bring their children home. The media sympathized with the families and wielded their influence as well. Every day, Canadian GLA families' stories were told on the local news broadcasts, and some even received national attention. The Canadian news crews also contacted us in Haiti and reported on the story from our perspective.

During this time, one of the youngest Canadian babies became seriously ill. Six-month-old Wilson had been brought to GLA with his twin brother, Mackenson, when they were only a few weeks old. Now Wilson was fighting for his life. After the earthquake there was more sickness than normal in the nurseries and, like so many other children, Wilson came down with a nasty strain of a stomach and intestinal bug. His was worse than most, though, requiring the use of IV fluids and antibiotics to get him hydrated and healthy again. After a few days of improvement, his symptoms came back, this time worse than ever. Wilson was dangerously dehydrated, unresponsive, and at one point he even stopped breathing. With as much sickness as we had been having, our medical supplies were running low, and we didn't have any more IV supplies, without which Wilson would surely die. That night the Dutch donations arrived, including those much-needed medical supplies. Wilson's collapsed veins from severe dehydration made starting the lifesaving IV a challenge, but with persistence, the nurses succeeded. We were still fighting, and Wilson was fighting, but we knew our supplies would run low again, and our needs were great. That made it all the more frustrating that the Canadian government seemed to be dragging their feet. Wilson needed medical care and, while we were doing everything we could, this was Haiti—post-earthquake Haiti at that—and we didn't have the resources of a developed nation. While the Canadian government was arguing and talking semantics, a little boy was struggling for his life. A struggle that didn't have to be as life-threatening as it currently was.

Then Wilson's story, including pictures of him sick, reached the Canadian people. Their hearts went out to the suffering child, and many more Canadians began calling for the evacuation of the children. With the media and the people of Canada rooting for evacuation, we hoped it was only a matter of time before the government would agree as well. We also hoped it would not be too late.

A few days later, we began hearing rumors of a possible evacuation, although there were many different stories and versions of this rumor, especially regarding exactly which children would be eligible. Léa had contacted the government for days before receiving a response, but finally they were giving some indication that an evacuation might be possible, at least for some of the children. We were fighting for all, but some would be better than none.

The government officials wanted to know details of how many children were in the process of adoption, though, and what stages they were in. A representative from the Canadian embassy first showed up at GLA on Friday, January 22, a week and a half after the earthquake. We had spent the past two days evacuating more than two-thirds of our children, and most of our staff was still in Miami, having just travelled there with the American children. The representative's arrival in the late afternoon was an unexpected surprise, since we had received virtually no communication from the Canadian embassy in Haiti.

We sat down with the representative and began to talk about the logistics of the evacuation. We were grateful and relieved to receive actual confirmation that the Canadian children would be able to evacuate, and sooner rather than later. The Canadian government would provide transportation, which was fine with us, as long as we were able to provide our own escorts to travel with the children. The representative readily agreed, admitting that they had a shortage of escorts and that would be helpful to them. There was a flight scheduled for the following evening, and she wanted to put our children on it. We told her that this would not be possible, because our staff members would not yet be back. We refused to send our children alone, especially without the opportunity for them and our staff members to say good-bye. We had seen the differences between the European evacuation, with the children travelling with strangers, and the American evacuation, where the children were only taken from the staff to be placed into their families. This was a better way, and it was what we were insisting on for our Canadian children. Since Wilson had stabilized and there was currently no physical threat to any of the children, their mental and emotional health was our top priority.

Although the embassy's representative was not happy with our decision, she accepted it, and told us there would be another flight Tuesday or Wednesday, and another a few days later. We promised to keep her informed as to when our staff would return, assuring her that we were eager for our kids to go home, as soon as we felt they could realistically do so.

After a few more logistical details were taken care of—names and passport numbers of prospective escorts who would travel with the children—the representative needed to see and photograph each child who would be evacuating to Canada. We went out back, where the kids and their nannies were all outside, and I helped her locate each child on her list. She snapped a quick photo for identification purposes until we had made it through all the children at the main house. We told her there were eleven kids at the main house and nine at the toddler house. She counted her pictures and was ready to head up the hill for the rest of the photos. Another staff member suggested double-checking the files, but the lady was in a hurry and didn't want to take the time.

I followed the representative to the car and climbed into the backseat. I gave the driver directions to the toddler house in Creole, a fact which didn't earn me any points with the embassy representative, who gave me a disapproving look when I told her I didn't speak French, and I sat in uncomfortable silence during the short drive up the mountain. When we arrived at the toddler house, it was shortly before sunset, and the kids were all outside playing. They were excited to greet another group of visitors, and quickly cooperated with the picture-taking process. We called the names of the Canadian children and they formed a line, standing quietly and smiling when it was their turn to get their photo taken. Some of the other kids were confused and didn't understand why they were not getting their picture taken, but even they weren't disruptive to the process, just curious. The only real problem was when four-year-old Moïse's file came up with his sister Nerline's file attached to it. They were the only set of Canadian siblings divided between the houses, and we had not taken her picture back at the main house.

Because the representative had to physically see and photograph each child, after all the pictures were taken at the toddler house, we had to return to the main house to take sweet Nerline's picture. The representative was not at all happy to be making another trip down the hill, now in the dark. She was also not pleased with me for my fault in this situation, and I think we were both relieved when she had taken her picture and was finally able to make her way back to the embassy. We at GLA were especially grateful for the promise of another evacuation.

From that point on, we believed that we would have a few days of simple packing and preparing, but we should have known better. Nothing had been easy about this evacuation, so why would that change now? The following day we received an email from the embassy regarding additional paperwork required for three of the children. One of their families' adoption documents had expired, and they would need to get them renewed . . . immediately. Their children would not be permitted to evacuate without this paperwork. I got in touch with the families, who quickly went about replacing the out-of-date document. Normally the process of getting new documents would have taken months, but this was an emergency situation and the respective government agencies processed the necessary paperwork in record time.

Not only were we busy with these logistical concerns, but the rumors and speculation had not gone away, either. We had been told that everyone would be evacuating, but our Canadian families were still hearing stories of lists of kids who could come and those who would stay. They had also heard that we had refused an evacuation flight, and some were led to believe that had been our only opportunity for evacuating the children. All these rumors and speculation were especially frustrating for us at GLA. The Canadian government had been extremely slow in contacting us in any way. They had shown no concern for the Canadian citizens in residence, let alone the adoptive children, yet now they were trying to pressure us into acting immediately, which we were in no position to do. We now had the Canadian government's approval to take the kids to Canada, and we would see that it was done. But it would be done on our judgment of when it was possible and when it would be in the children's best interest for the smoothest transition we could provide.

We received emails from several of the parents, and Léa, our liaison in Canada, heard from so many nervous and confused parents, each with a slightly different version of the story, that she called GLA to learn what we knew. She and I had a long conversation about exactly what had and had not been said by the embassy representative. I assured her that we had been promised that our kids could travel on the first flight out, once our staff in Miami had returned. We were not being careless or trying to cause additional delay and worry for the parents; we were looking out for the children's best interest. We simply didn't have the staff in Haiti to prepare and transport the children to the airport, much less travel with them to Canada. We wanted the children evacuated, but we wanted it done properly. Léa understood our concerns and our reasoning, and she did her best to pass along those reassurances to the families.

Fortunately, the travelling staff members arrived back as scheduled, returning to GLA late Monday night. They were relieved to finally be back in Haiti, although they were weary from their travelling and the stress of the past few days. Laurie and I were also thankful to see them. It had been a long few days without them, and we were more than ready to relinquish responsibility for the orphanage. Everyone knew that their stay would not be long, though, since we had received a tentative plan for the Canadian children to fly out on Wednesday.

It was around this time that we collectively started to feel the strain of the days since the earthquake. Our bodies could only run on adrenaline for so long, and they were starting to wear down. We were physically drained, after working long days with little sleep under stressful circumstances. We were emotionally exhausted from saying good-bye to the children we loved, seeing the destruction of the country we had come to call home, and knowing the desperate plight of the Haitian people. There had been no time to sit and truly process the tragedy that had happened or to try to make sense of any of it.

Besides all that, we were still living in uncertainty. The aftershocks, while not as strong or frequent as the first few days, were still fairly constant. Every day we had between one and four officially registered aftershocks of magnitude 4.0 or higher, with even more smaller shocks and the rocking motion of the earth. We vacillated between fear, anger, and annoyance with the aftershocks, but always there was a response, both physical and emotional. We were all on the same side, but the fight was taking its toll. Our tempers were running short and our patience was wearing thin. Our emotions were raw.

Knowing we would not have the full staff in Haiti for long, we took advantage of the opportunity to regroup before preparing for the next evacuation. Laurie and I apprised Dixie of the most urgent situations requiring her attention, including several we had been unable to take care of without her. The returning staff members unpacked and then repacked for the next journey. They also did what they could to prepare the children for evacuation and the orphanage for their further absence.

We gathered supplies for yet another group of evacuating children. By this time we knew the routine, knew what to take and how to pack it. The problem was that we were also running out of clothes, especially warmer clothes and shoes and socks. We did the best we could, packed blankets, and hoped that the parents would understand the circumstances and anticipate their children's need for warmer clothing once they arrived.

As we went about our work on Tuesday, we kept one ear tuned to the phone. We knew the evacuation flight was planned for Wednesday, and the Canadian embassy had said they would call with details on Tuesday. It was late afternoon when they called, and they did confirm a Wednesday morning flight for our Canadian evacuees and escorts. What was unexpected was that they were requiring everyone to come spend Tuesday night at the Canadian embassy, from where they would be transported to the airport the next morning. We were expected to be at the embassy by 6:00 p.m. None of us were happy about this decision, but we knew we had no say in the matter. The next hour or two were frantically spent with final packing for this latest turn of events. We made last-minute preparations for the children, and the staff members got ready to leave GLA again, not even a full day after arriving back in Haiti.

Soon the main house children who were headed to Canada were seated in a neat row on the couches downstairs. They looked around with confusion, curiosity, and suspicion. They didn't know what was happening. The Canadian kids from the toddler house joined them on the nearby dining room chairs, since the couches were full.

While the adults finished their last-minute preparations, the children waited patiently, though many of the younger ones squirmed and fidgeted. Many of the children understood that it was their turn to evacuate, although they didn't really understand what that meant. What they did know was that soon they would be with their moms and dads in their forever families. That was enough to help them through the process, but not to remove all their anxiety. It was a big change, and they did understand that.

By the time of the Canadian evacuation, I had become numb to the grief. It was not that I didn't care about the children leaving that day, but my tears and emotional vulnerability had been shoved behind a protective wall that was growing ever stronger in my heart. I was afraid that if I let the full force of my grief seek expression, I would drown in the pain.

I said good-bye to each of the twenty children and kissed them one last time as they and their escorts loaded into vans. The heavy numbness stayed in my heart as they began the trek down the mountain, the first step on their journey toward their new lives.

CHAPTER 16

MONTREAL OR OTTAWA

The LORD is a refuge for the oppressed,
A stronghold in times of trouble.
Those who know your name will trust in you,
For you, LORD, have never forsaken those who seek you.

~ Psalm 9:9–10

ANOTHER EVACUATION, ANOTHER GOOD-BYE, ANOTHER
caravan down the mountain. The scene was familiar, though no
two evacuations were the same. This time the trip would be shorter,
as they were not going directly to the airport, but to the Canadian
embassy near Petionville. Spending the night at the embassy was
surprising enough, but even more so since we had heard that ninety
percent of the building was uninhabitable. Why, then, did they want
our children to stay there, and would they be safe?

Fortunately, the travelers soon learned that, while the embassy
building had sustained structural damage in parts, most of the damage was broken glass and debris that had not yet been cleaned, and

this is what had earned many areas the label "condemned." There was plenty of space for the evacuees outside in the courtyard and in one of the administrative areas inside. They would be safe there.

At this point, even after the children had left GLA, there was still confusion among the Canadian families as to where their children would be arriving the next day. We had been told the evacuation would be to Ottawa, but some of the families were hearing from their contacts that the children would be flown to Montreal, more than one hundred miles away. There were many emails and phone calls exchanged that night, and ultimately each family made their own decision as to where they would travel. We could only pray that when the plane landed, all of the families would be at the airport to meet their children.

The Caribbean sun had already set by the time the children and their escorts arrived at the Canadian embassy in Haiti. Although it was dark, it would still be hours until the children's bedtime, so most of the group stayed outside where chairs had been set up in the courtyard. The strange circumstances and confusion kept many of the children close to the adults they knew and trusted, but a few were braver: they ran off to play, explore the paved courtyard, and climb the steps that led to the embassy's entrance. The weary adults did their best to keep everyone occupied, happy, and safe.

As the children's bedtime approached, the kids were moved inside, to the small room they would be sharing with those from other orphanages who would be evacuating with them on their flight the next day. Thin mattresses lined the floor. Sleeping on the floor was becoming common for the children and even some of the adults. They wrapped themselves in the blankets the embassy staff had given them to ward off the chill of the air conditioning and, those who were able, slept. Throughout the night the scene varied little, with a few children awake, too out of sorts with their surroundings to give in to sleep. Several of the adults were similarly restless, even more so because of their responsibility for the children. They did what they could for them: rubbing backs, giving reassuring hugs, and doing their best not to look too deeply into the dark alcove stacked with body bags, a gruesome reminder of the Canadian embassy's own losses in the past weeks. The children were too young to notice or understand their significance, but the adults shied away from that area. It was a long night with very little rest, especially for those caring for the youngest children. The unfamiliar environment had taken its toll and they were fussy and cranky and needing love and reassurance. They had no way to comprehend what was going on around them, much less process it into anything that made sense of their world. In spite of the little-to-no-sleep some of the adults had received, they were all relieved when morning's light appeared and they could quit pretending or trying to sleep.

The morning routine kept everyone busy changing diapers and taking older children to the bathroom. Then the children were changed into clean clothes to meet their parents. After a breakfast of peanut butter sandwiches, it was time to head to the airport. The children and adults, with all of their luggage, were loaded onto buses and escorted by the Canadian military down to the airport. The familiar landmarks were gone, but those who had travelled this route several times in the past week were beginning to recognize new landmarks in the fallen buildings, and in the streets and parks taken over by tents and large piles of debris and rubble. It was disconcerting how quickly our worst nightmare had become our normal frame of reference. It was the children's first trip into the city, but they didn't seem any more fazed than the other evacuated children had when it was their turn to travel to the airport.

The evacuation routine was also becoming familiar as, a short time later, GLA staff and volunteers were once again loading children onto the airplane, making sure each child had the proper supervision. A team of Canadian medical personnel had checked each child and approved all of them for travel, so there were no hindrances there. The only real hitch came when they were not allowed to load their luggage on board the plane with the children. Medical supplies and soy formula were in those bags, and now they were inaccessible in the cargo hold. The older children were fed onboard from cardboard boxes of macaroni and cheese, and the babies were given formula, but those with milk allergies had only water. It was certainly not what we had planned for the children but, like so many things, it was out of our control. The staff had to make the best of their circumstances, however much they would have preferred better for these children.

Four and a half hours after taking off from Port-au-Prince, the airplane touched down in Ottawa, Canada. The travelers had expected cold weather, but the blast of frigid air that met them at the exit to the plane was still a shock. The Canadian Red Cross was prepared for their arrival and met them with warm blankets that they wrapped around everyone as they prepared to disembark. The blankets made the trek down the stairs and across the runway cumbersome, but no one wanted to face the cold without them. The staff and children then entered the hangar, ready to meet the parents and unite them with their children.

While the children and staff had been making their trip, the parents had faced entirely different journeys to bring them to this reunion. Although Edward and Sarah had only recently been matched with eighteen-month-old twins Kesnel and Fresnel, their adoption story was much longer and had been littered with ups and downs that were culminating in this dream come true.

After the adoption of their daughter from GLA several years earlier, Edward and Sarah knew they wanted to adopt again, so they went through the process of filling out the paperwork and meeting with social workers and everything else necessary for an adoption from Haiti. Their file was completed and sent off in the fall of 2007, but they never received word from GLA that it had arrived. Eventually the file was found, but their adoption agency had accidentally sent it to Hong Kong instead of Haiti. By the time their paperwork was retrieved and arrived at GLA, they had faced several more months of fruitless waiting. Finally, near the end of 2008, Edward and Sarah were matched with a little boy, and they looked forward to welcoming him into their family. Only two months later, however, the child they had come to love as their son was returned to his birth family when his mother changed her mind about giving him up for adoption.

It was a difficult time for Edward and Sarah as they grieved their loss. They felt God moving them to adopt from a different country, so they withdrew their file from GLA and began the process of redoing the paperwork for the African nation they had selected. They were excited and hopeful until they learned that the program they were interested in no longer adopted children to Canada. At that point, they were devastated and confused. They didn't want their daughter to grow up an only child, and they wanted more children. They knew there were children needing the family and love they were wanting to provide. Yet with every move they made, another door slammed in their faces.

Edward and Sarah wondered why things were happening this way and they prayed about what to do next. They contacted GLA again, and they also decided to try to adopt siblings. Within a month of their file arriving back in Haiti, Edward and Sarah were matched with Kesnel and Fresnel in December 2009.

Exactly two weeks after receiving their proposal, the earthquake struck Haiti, and their doubts and questions returned. What was going to happen now? What would this mean for their adoption? Was this another dead end? There were also the obvious concerns for their sons' health and safety in such an unstable Haiti. Although the connection was new, they loved these two boys and were not going to give up without a fight. Like so many other parents, they worked to raise awareness of their children's situation and petitioned for them to be allowed to come home.

A week after the earthquake, the Canadian government announced they would be fast-tracking the adoptions in progress, but Edward and Sarah still didn't know what that meant for them, since they were so early in the process. Did their adoption count as in progress since it had not even entered the Haitian social service office yet? Fortunately, it did, and on January 21 they officially learned that Kesnel and Fresnel would be a part of the Canadian evacuation, whenever it took place.

Their social worker advised Edward and Sarah to get to Montreal as quickly as possible, since no one seemed to know exactly when the children would be arriving. They booked the necessary flights, but a winter snowstorm caused the cancellation of those flights and made it difficult to reschedule. After that delay, they made it to Montreal and began the wait for their children's evacuation. The next day, an immigration official called to inform them the children would be arriving in Ottawa, not Montreal, so they would need to make another trip. Edward and Sarah took a train on what they hoped would be the final leg of their journey to meet up with their boys.

Finally the plane was coming and it was time to gather at the airport. Edward and Sarah met many of the other GLA parents among the group waiting in the airport hangar. Like the American families had experienced in Miami, many of these parents had connected online and now knew each other, even though they had never before met in person. It was an exciting time as the parents met face to face, and especially as they waited for the arrival of their children. Everyone was happy and smiling and talking and laughing and (especially) watching the window where they would be able to see the plane land. As the time of the children's arrival drew nearer, the parents moved closer and closer toward the window until everyone was crowded around it. Outside in the cold, they could see the reporters who were also waiting on the plane's arrival, but they were not allowed inside the room where the parents were waiting. When the plane arrived, it stopped on the tarmac just outside the window, and the parents watched as the door opened and adults climbed down the steps carrying blanket-clad children off the plane.

Now everyone crowded the door, anxious to meet their children as they were being brought into the room a few at a time. Each child's name was called, and the eager parents stepped out of the crowd.

When Fresnel's name was called, Edward and Sarah rushed forward to meet him. They took turns holding him and playing with him with smiles on their faces and joy in their hearts. They waited for Kesnel, but when no one brought him inside, they asked a volunteer where he was and were directed to the medical bus set up outside. Kesnel had diarrhea on the plane, so they wanted to make sure he was okay before they sent him home. After he had been examined and released, Edward and Sarah took Kesnel and Fresnel back to the main room while they waited their turn to clear immigration.

The boys were happy and adventurous, content to explore their surroundings and play, especially with the toy cars. They loved taking cuddle breaks with their new parents, but the boys were lively and full of energy and soon ready to get back to their play. Edward and Sarah were ecstatic, their hearts overflowing with the joy they felt at watching their new sons, knowing there was no more waiting. This was God's plan for them, and it was so much more beautiful than they could have imagined.

Things only got better when they finally made it home, and their daughter met her new brothers. It was love at first sight, and she played with them and followed them around as they climbed over all the furniture. With a big smile on her face, Angie turned to her parents and asked, "Can we keep them?"

PART III

LIFE AFTER THE EARTHQUAKE AND EVACUATION

CHAPTER 17

A FEW OF THE MASSES

Whoever welcomes one of these little children
in my name welcomes me;
and whoever welcomes me does not welcome me
but the one who sent me.

~ Mark 9:37

AFTER THE CANADIAN CHILDREN EVACUATED, only the French children were left. We were still working for their evacuation, but at the moment the French government was only allowing those with completed adoptions to go home.

Our primary purpose in evacuating the children had been to get them out of the uncertainties of Haiti and unite them with their families; a secondary purpose was to have the time and resources to help children outside our own walls. With so many beds now empty, we could take in some of the countless children we knew were in need.

Jude was the first child to arrive at GLA after the earthquake. He was two weeks old and weighed just over three pounds when we first met him, the day of the American children's evacuation. While the evacuees were waiting at the airport that day, relief workers from a mission in Port-au-Prince brought the tiny baby to them, asking for help. Dixie and Susan examined baby Jude who was, at least, breathing steadily. While he didn't appear to be in any immediate danger, Jude was clearly malnourished and dehydrated, and he had a low body temperature. The medical workers with the mission had done their best to care for him by giving him fluids, but they lacked the necessary resources to care for one so small. They wanted our staff to take him to the USA for medical treatment, but Dixie refused, explaining that even under these emergency circumstances he could not evacuate without the necessary paperwork. They agreed to transfer Jude to our care, since we were much better equipped to care for premature and underweight babies.

Jude had been born to a nineteen-year-old orphan, a single mother whose boyfriend had left her for another woman when she became pregnant. Jude's father ultimately died before his son was born. It was impossible for our staff to know how far along in her pregnancy Marie Noel had been when she gave birth to Jude, but it appeared that he had been born prematurely.

Life was hard for Marie Noel as she tried to provide for her fragile son without the support of a family of her own. Tiny Jude struggled to feed, he didn't gain weight, and then he became ill. Just when it seemed impossible for life to get any harder, Marie Noel and Jude experienced the earthquake on January 12. If she had had friends and neighbors to turn to before, she didn't now. It was a time of chaos and uncertainty. The world was in upheaval, and the people around her were spending all their available energy trying to piece their own lives together again. There was shelter to find, family members to search for, and the lost to bury and mourn. They needed food and water for themselves and their families, and they didn't have the time, energy, or resources to help the young mother and her newborn son.

With the arrival of the hordes of emergency relief workers, Jude's mother found a thread of hope. Marie Noel, recognizing her own inability to help her son, turned to the strangers. Foreign missionaries and aid workers were a common and permanent fixture in Haiti, and with the ground still shaking with regular aftershocks, these foreigners were more prevalent than ever. Everyone knew of Haiti's need, and the world was reaching out to do what it could for the devastated island nation. Marie Noel took her infant and did what she believed would get her son the attention he needed to survive: she abandoned him. Marie Noel placed Jude on a dirt pile and walked away, but she only went a short distance, then waited and watched until someone found Jude. As expected, a group of people with white faces wearing medical scrubs soon came by and took the child into their care. The team of medical aid workers had come to Haiti to help with earthquake relief, and they could tell that this child needed immediate medical attention. When they returned to the clinic, Marie Noel followed them and explained her situation. She asked them to take care of him, to make him healthy and strong, and to provide a future for him. They agreed to do what they could for Jude. With that assurance—but empty arms—Marie Noel headed back to the tent that was now all she had to call home.

Jude, meanwhile, was already being treated by the medical team. As a premature infant, he had been born small, but he had not grown and was becoming emaciated and dehydrated. The team started an IV and gave him fluids, but they recognized that they could not properly care for Jude. There were many needs in Haiti at the time, and they were ill-equipped to provide the necessary attention and treatment to a premature baby. This recognition brought them to the airport the day of our American evacuation.

There was little our nurses could do for him while still at the airport, but they made sure he was kept warm and fed throughout the day. After the long wait was over and the American children and their escorts were on their way to Miami, Jude made the trip to GLA with our volunteers who were not making the trip to the US. It had been a long day, and most of the volunteers who were now travelling back up the mountain to GLA with baby Jude had arrived in Haiti only two days earlier. Several of these volunteers were nurses, so they were eager to do what they could for the struggling infant. Jude had already proven he was a fighter: he was a three-pound baby who had made it to two weeks old with minimal medical assistance. At such a young age, he had also survived the earthquake, but a healing wound on his face showed that he had not done so without injury.

Once they arrived back at GLA, the three nurses immediately set to work properly caring for Jude. He was placed in an incubator to help keep his body temperature at a healthy level, and the nurses started an IV line to rehydrate him and a feeding tube, since he had difficulty sucking properly from a bottle. Not until they were confident they had done everything possible did they quit for the night and go to bed, leaving Jude under the watchful eye of the overnight Haitian nannies.

Early the next morning, the nurses who had brought Jude up the mountain returned to check on him in the NICU nursery. Jude was a demanding baby, requiring a lot of time and attention, but our volunteer nurses were more than willing to do what was necessary. They held him close, loved him, and gave him the attention he needed. They worked hard to coax him to feed, little by little, teaching him to suck so he could take his food orally rather than through the tube. It soon became apparent that Jude had an infection in addition to his malnutrition and dehydration. He had diarrhea and began having seizures. The diarrhea made the task of rehydrating and nourishing him that much harder, and the seizures required a whole new level of treatment. The nurses had different backgrounds—in intensive care, pediatric nursing, and rural medicine—that worked well together and allowed them unique insights into the situation. When none of them knew what to do, they sought outside help from doctors back home, pediatricians who specialized in neo-natal care. Laurie and I were always willing to let them use the telephone to seek help for our newest child. As an added bonus, a busy line meant no incoming media calls we had to answer.

Gradually, one precious step at a time, Jude began to get better, recovering from both his life-threatening malnutrition and the infection that had plagued him on his arrival. Jude became a welcome part of our lives, and he continued to grow and get stronger in the care of our nurses and nannies.

Even though I had nothing to do with the care of Jude, he was a symbol of hope. He arrived at GLA when I was suffering most and things seemed darkest. In the previous forty-eight hours, more than one hundred children had left us, and my heart was bruised. I knew, however, that there were so many more children out there, suffering and in need because of the earthquake, and I was eager to help them as well. Jude was the promise that we would get that chance, that we would be able to help some of the many we knew were in desperate need during those days. We wanted to help with earthquake relief in the way we knew best, by taking care of some of Haiti's most vulnerable: her children. We could not heal ourselves, but perhaps we could help them heal.

Harry was the next child to come to GLA; he was a boy of about nine or ten years old. His house had collapsed during the earthquake, killing his father and injuring Harry when a wall fell on him. Harry's mother took him to the hospital, but as she also had a younger son to care for, she was unable to stay with him. The hospital transferred Harry to the USNS Comfort, the US Navy's medical relief vessel just offshore, where his injuries were treated. When they were ready to release Harry, no one knew where he was from or how to find his family, so the ship staff released him into the care of another mission. That mission was already overwhelmed with helping their local community, though, so they asked us to take him in.

Harry travelled up the mountain to GLA with our staff when they arrived back in Haiti from escorting the American children to Miami. His injuries were no longer critical, but his left arm was bandaged and he was unable or unwilling to bear weight on his left leg. It was a painful trip for Harry, as each of the hundreds of bumps jolted his injured hip and brought a wince or a gasp of pain from the young boy. Eventually Harry found relief in sleep. Although he was recovering well, Harry's injuries would require ongoing care.

In addition to caring for Harry physically, we also took on the responsibility of finding his mother and reuniting him with his family. This was not as outrageous a claim as it might seem for an orphanage that typically processed foreign adoptions. Actually, it was something we were uniquely equipped to do, since during the course of a child's adoption it was sometimes necessary for us to find missing biological parents who were required to appear before the courts to relinquish custody. In those cases, we worked with investigators who would track down the parents for us, and we trusted that those relationships would prove useful in this case as well. We began conversations with administration at the hospital ship about an ongoing partnership with them. They could release more children to us, ones like Harry who had no place to go. We had the capability to care for them, including treating any ongoing medical needs, until we were able to reunite them with whatever biological family members they had left. We were excited about the possibility of being able to help with such an important part of the earthquake's aftermath: reuniting displaced children with their families.

In the chaos and bustle that followed Harry's arrival, I didn't immediately become acquainted with him: no more than cursory interactions when my responsibilities took me into the nurseries. At least, the chaos and bustle were the excuses I made to myself for not seeking him out, and there is no doubt that we were busy. The real truth, however, is that I was scared. I was emotionally raw, and I had not yet learned how healing it would be to spend time with a child who had suffered through incredible loss, yet who still had the capacity to smile and laugh and love.

I first truly met Harry two days after his arrival, when an inspector from a government agency came by, wanting information about our orphanage and the children there. The representative asked to see Harry, and I carried him down from the nurseries. I had known of Harry's major injuries, but I hadn't realized until he was in my arms how many more minor scratches and scrapes covered his body. These injuries were not as dramatic as his others, but in their own way they were a more powerful testimony to the damage the earthquake had done to him. That encounter shook me, especially as I looked at Harry's smile and marveled at his strength.

Later that same day we received another displaced child, a five-year-old girl named Charline. Like Harry, Charline came from the USNS Comfort, but she had been released directly into our care, and she had traveled up to GLA with our driver and an emergency volunteer who had gone with him to retrieve her. Upon her arrival, Charline was brought into the office where I was working. She had a small garbage bag of treasures with her, stuffed animals and treats that the staff of the Comfort had given her. Charline also had a handwritten note telling her story. She had been taken to the Red Cross by her papa, and from there she had been transferred to the Comfort. Her note gave the names of family members, the school she attended, and the church where the Red Cross had admitted her for care. Having had no such information to help us locate Harry's mother, and no real leads in finding her, we were optimistic that Charline's family would be easier to find.

Also like Harry, Charline had innumerable cuts, bruises, and scrapes all over her body. Her most serious injury was a deep gash on the top of her foot. It was healing nicely, but would require continual bandaging and ongoing care to insure that it didn't become infected.

When I asked the obvious question—if something had fallen on her foot to cause the injury—Charline nodded and showed me another injury, a scar on her head. I asked what had fallen on her, and she said simply, *lakay*—"the house." Hearing such a story told so matter-of-factly was heartbreaking. At such a young age, Charline had lived through things no one should have to endure. And to know that her story was only one of millions was overwhelming, especially considering that she was one of the lucky ones.

In many ways it was those children who came after the evacuations, the ones who needed us, who began to help us heal. They didn't take the place of the children we had lost; those were scars that would take time to heal and holes that no one could fill. Even so, the love of these new children who, like us, had also experienced loss, was a balm to our wounded souls. We loved the French children who were still with us, but they were a reminder of our own pain and loss. I could not look at them without seeing the faces that should have been beside them. The displaced children brought us outside of ourselves and our own pain and face to face with the hurt of others. Knowing they would not be staying with us long-term made it easier to open our hearts to them. They would not be unexpectedly taken away from us; we knew they were leaving, and the sooner for them the better. Not only that, but helping them freed us from a feeling of helplessness, of uselessness in Haiti. We were in the middle of a disaster zone, but these were the first victims outside our own walls whom we had been able to help in a personal way.

Harry and Charline quickly settled in and began to feel at home at GLA. Because of his injuries, Harry was unable to get out of bed by himself and was dependent on someone taking him wherever he wanted to go. Charline, on the other hand, quickly learned her way around the nurseries and the rest of the house. She didn't like to stay in the nurseries with the rest of the kids, but would usually show up wherever she thought the most interesting things were going on. Sometimes she joined me in the office, sitting on my lap while I worked on my daily tasks. More often she went to the common room, where the volunteers were gathered, confident that she would get their full and undivided attention.

Harry was small for his age, and he was a bright boy with a huge heart. In spite of the tragedy and personal trauma he had lived through, Harry had a great sense of humor and he loved to laugh. Just hearing Harry laugh was enough to brighten my day, and spending time with him helped me forget everything else that was going on around us and our own daily struggles. Harry was sensitive and loving and kind, and he brought joy into our lives.

Charline had a spirit that was infectious and a personality that made her seem older than her five years. She was outgoing and friendly, eager to love and be loved. She could be stubborn and demanding at times, but she was so exuberant and vivacious that no one seemed able to deny her anything she wanted.

When Harry and Charline arrived, we also had the children from the toddler house staying with us. There were only a few kids left there—three French children and two children of GLA nannies who had lost their homes—so it didn't make sense for them to stay at the toddler house while GLA staff was out of the country escorting the evacuated children home. These kids were more used to our structure and rules, and they stayed in the nursery unless invited out by volunteers or staff. It didn't take long, however, until the volunteers began bringing Harry and the toddler house kids downstairs to join them and Charline, and they would all spend their days together. The older children even began eating some of their meals with us at the long table downstairs, which was usually overflowing with people, but was now less than half-full.

On one such afternoon, I took a break from my work and joined the volunteers and kids in the common room. They had clearly been having a party of sorts and everyone was smiling and happy. Charline, both the newest and the most outgoing member of the group, showed me the temporary tattoo the volunteers had put on her arm. She also showed me the tattoo on the girl next to her and told me that all the other kids had gotten them as well. Charline teased that I didn't have one, and I pretended to pout and cry. Harry, who had cuddled up on my lap when I came into the room, didn't want me to feel left out, so he decided to cheer me up. He took the stickers off his face—a favorite place for Haitian children to put their stickers—and started decorating my face with them. Harry didn't stop until I was wearing every one of his stickers. He refused to take even a single one back. That act of generosity and his accompanying grin stole my heart that day.

When Charline came downstairs by herself, she especially enjoyed looking at pictures or videos on our computers. One time she was watching a video of the recently evacuated American children as they sat and sang together, while waiting during the interminable hours the evacuation had taken. Charline began talking to the computer screen, saying "Hey! Hey!" and trying to get the attention of one of the adults in the video whom she recognized. I tried explaining to Charline that it was a video of things that had happened previously and that the people in the video could not see her now. "Oh, yes, they can!" Charline argued, "She sees me. She keeps looking at me!" Charline pointed out one of the older girls in the group who, in fact, kept looking at the camera. I tried explaining one more time what was really going on. Charline didn't argue, but she also didn't believe me.

Although they were generally happy and teasing children, Harry and Charline did have their struggles. Not only had they lived through the earthquake, but that disaster had separated them from their families. By the time they arrived at GLA, they had already been apart from them for nearly two weeks. Harry would sometimes get quiet and sad, and Charline often asked me if we had found her papa yet.

Both Harry and Charline loved us and we loved them, but we could not replace the parents they had lost. Nor did we want to. What we wanted was to find their families, but that task was proving harder than we had hoped.

Our staff members had visited General Hospital, where Harry's mother had taken him, several times since he arrived. They took pictures of Harry with them and showed them to the staff there. The hospital building had been severely damaged in the earthquake, however, and the hospital administration was busy and chaotic, staffed mostly by an ever-changing regime of foreign humanitarians trying to care for the needs of the injured masses. They had no form of re-cord-keeping, and no one recognized Harry's picture. It was unlikely that any of them had even been there when he had been admitted, and our inquiries were fruitless and frustrating.

Our staff had also visited the school and church indicated on Charline's note, but they had not had any more success with that search. The school was able to direct them to her family's neighborhood, but no one was living there anymore or able to help in the search. They spoke to the pastor at the church, and he promised to make an announcement in the service on Sunday. But Sunday came and went, and still we had no word.

Dixie and the other staff members had returned from the Canadian evacuation over the weekend, so on Monday she began working on new tactics for finding Harry and Charline's families. She asked me to make posters with Harry's name and picture and GLA's contact information. I made the posters and, although I understood the need for them, it felt wrong, as though I was making "Wanted" posters or signs for a lost dog. It reminded me of how the Dutch children had looked like refugees and how our feelings didn't change our reality—as much as we loved these children, their situation was desperate. Once my posters were done, Dixie and our driver took them down to the hospital and posted them wherever they could, in the hopes that Harry's mom was looking for him there. She also contacted the radio station with information about Charline, asking them to please announce that Charline was at GLA and that we were looking for her family. We didn't know if these new ventures would work, but it did feel good to be trying something other than the same futile attempts we had been making.

Harry's mother had, in fact, been returning to the hospital, but she met the same challenges we did and no one could tell her where her son had gone or how she could find him. It was discouraging work, but she had not given up. Then, the very day after we had hung Harry's picture on the wall, his mother walked in to see his familiar face smiling back at her. She was overjoyed and immediately called the number listed, not taking her eyes off her son's precious face until she was sure she knew where he was and how to get there.

Meanwhile, Harry had been taken a few miles up the road to another hospital. He was doing well, but still refused to bear weight on his left leg and winced any time one of the nurses forced him to try. They believed that it was a reaction to the memory of pain rather than any physical problem with the leg. However, to be safe, they had sent him to get x-rayed. Harry had been taken to the hospital before his mother called, and he was still gone when she arrived a short while later.

It was a long wait for Harry's mother, knowing he was so close, yet still out of reach. When Harry returned to GLA, his mother was one of the first people he saw as the vehicle pulled in the gate. She was sitting there, in our yard, waiting for him. The huge smiles that lit up both their faces when they saw each other were priceless; it was easy to see how very happy they were to be united again. Whenever you asked Harry who she was, a bright smile lit up his face as he said, *maman mwen!*—"my mother!" They had been separated for nearly three full weeks, but now they were together again and at peace.

Originally our medical staff had told Harry's mother that he was not strong enough to leave and that we needed to keep him with us a little longer, but she insisted on taking him home with her. His brother had been asking for Harry and wanted to see him. With all the loss she had already suffered, she wanted her family together again. We couldn't argue with that reasoning and, after all, the x-rays showed that no bones were broken. Harry's muscles and soft tissue were simply bruised and needed time and strengthening. So with lots of instructions and demonstrations on proper care and exercise, Harry was given permission to go home. We gave them medicine for Harry's injuries and basic relief supplies—a tarp, blankets, and rice. We said good-bye to a very happy Harry and his equally ecstatic mother, and together they walked out the GLA gate.

Such an exciting reunion was a beautiful way to mark the third week since the earthquake. In the middle of all the tragedy and suffering and our own stress, we were thankful for this brief reminder of the beauty of love and family. It also gave us hope that life did go on and would continue to do so. The challenges we faced today would not always be with us. Maybe someday (and we hoped it would be soon) we would find our way out of our current struggles.

For at least one person at GLA, however, Harry's home going was not a reason for celebration. For Charline, Harry's leaving was the end of believing in her own reunion; it was the end of her hope.

From the time Charline had arrived, we had told her that we were looking for her father and that we were going to find him for her. Whenever we talked about her papa, she got a longing look deep in her eyes. It was obvious she and her father were close and that she loved him very much.

The first few days she was with us, Charline asked often if her papa was coming, and if we had found him. Charline had many friends and a lot of love at GLA, but she was homesick. Everything in this little girl's life had changed so quickly and drastically, and she just wanted to get back to what she knew and to those she loved most. After several days of disappointing answers, Charline had stopped asking when her papa was coming. We continued to reassure her that we were looking, but our inability to find him began to wear on her.

After Harry went home, Charline gave up entirely. "You don't have to look for my papa anymore. I want to stay here," she told me later that day. While it was nice to know that she was enjoying her time with us, staying long term had never been our plan for her. She was a child who had a loving family, and our desire was to reunite them. I believe Charline's desire to stay had less to do with us than it did with her fear and hopelessness. She no longer believed, or was afraid to believe, that we would find her father. It was easier for her to accept it if she was the one doing the rejecting. We began to pray harder than ever that we would find her father, and soon!

The very next day, Charline's papa called. He had heard her name on the radio and so learned that his precious daughter was with us. It was too late in the day for him to make the long trip up the mountain and back home before dark, but he said he would come to get Charline the next day. As soon as I was sure of the facts, I told Charline that we had found her papa and that he was coming to get her. After a momentary light flashed in her eyes, they darkened and she turned away from me, saying *se pa vre*—"it isn't true." I assured her that her father had called and talked to our Haitian administrator, that she could go ask for herself if she wanted. I told her that her father would be coming tomorrow to take her home. As I explained all this to Charline, I saw the hope growing in her eyes. She still denied believing me, but for the rest of the day she could not stop smiling.

Early the next morning, Charline's papa came through the gate at GLA. Charline saw him from an upstairs window, called out to him and came flying downstairs. Once she got outside, however, she got a bit shy and started crying, overwhelmed with emotions that a five-year-old was not equipped to handle. She was, after all, only a little girl: a little girl who had lost her family and home and so much else in the past few weeks. Her papa was sweet and gentle, pulling her into his arms and reassuring her that he really was there and that he was going to take her home. He held her while she grieved the losses she had both experienced and feared. Charline was so happy to see him again, though, and soon she was smiling and dancing with excitement. She proudly introduced her papa to her friends, and there was no more hesitation or fear in her smile.

Charline and her papa visited with each other and with us for a while before they left. We made sure he understood how to care for the injury on her foot, which was still healing, and we gave them food and relief supplies. By the time the two of them left together, Charline was practically skipping out the gate, showing no regret at leaving the place she once claimed she wanted to call home. We knew that, like too many others in Port-au-Prince, Charline—and Harry—would be sleeping outdoors under a tarp. But now she was with her family: she was going home. Our big fancy house with all its fun toys could not compare to the love and security of family.

Especially optimistic after our success at reuniting Harry and Charline with their families, we were eager to begin again with more children, but that opportunity never came. By that time, power had shifted in Haiti, and UNICEF, who was controlling much of Haitian social services in actuality if not in name, didn't want to put displaced children into orphanages that typically processed adoptions. They expressed fears that we would sell or traffic the children, rather than properly unify them with their biological families.

Baby Jude remained at GLA, where he continued to grow and get stronger. After he had been with us a couple of weeks, his mother came to visit. Marie Noel had returned to the mission that had taken Jude and said that she was reconsidering her decision to give up her son. She thought that once he was bigger and healthy enough she might be able to care for him. Staff at that mission brought her to us where she visited Jude and spoke with our administrators.

Uniting families, biological or adoptive, was ultimately our mission at GLA, and whenever possible we wanted to keep biological families together. However, Marie Noel had previously chosen to give Jude up, and we wanted to make sure she was serious about raising him. We didn't want her to decide it was too hard once he was again in her care and so bring him back to us or to another orphanage. We wanted what was best for Jude.

At the time of Marie Noel's visit, Jude was much better and his condition was no longer critical, but he was still too small and fragile to leave. Dixie invited Marie Noel to come live at GLA with Jude. She would be able to help care for her son, as well as learn parenting skills and basic childcare from our nannies and staff. Marie Noel accepted that offer, but was only with us for about a week before she became physically violent with our staff and was asked to leave.

During his time at GLA, Jude had several recurrences of serious illnesses common to children who have suffered malnutrition, and therefore lack the strength of children who have never known true hunger. Our staff nursed him through all his illnesses, though, and several months later he was strong enough, big enough, and healthy enough to return to the care of his mother, who had remained steadfast in her desire to raise her son. It had been a long road for both of them, and for all of us at GLA, but finally Jude was home. Finally, all of our displaced children were with their families.

CHAPTER 18

THE REMNANT AND
THOSE WHO CAME

But let all who take refuge in you be glad;

let them ever sing for joy.

Spread your protection over them,

That those who love your name may rejoice in you.

~ Psalm 5:11

BY THE BEGINNING OF FEBRUARY, we were becoming increasingly frustrated with the French government. They still had not authorized the evacuation of their adopted children. Instead, they reviewed each child's file individually before determining if he or she would be allowed to go home. We had been hearing for some time that three-year-old Micherline would be able to evacuate, but still there were no details as to when that would be. Micherline's legal adoption was complete, and she was only lacking her Haitian passport and French visa, travel papers which seemed an unnecessary formality in the chaos of our world. Finally, early in the second week of February, we received instructions to bring Micherline at noon the next day to the rendezvous point with the French embassy.

So on February 9, four weeks after the earthquake, I escorted Micherline to the Lysee Francais, the same school in Petionville where I had taken Daniel and Josef just over two weeks earlier. The road was the same, but there had been many changes. Much of the rubble and debris had been, if not entirely cleared away, at least contained in specific areas. The damaged portions of houses were being repaired or torn down, and the road was more passable. There was visible progress.

When we arrived at the school, I felt confident that I would have all the information they needed, since I had made careful notes and had collected the information I had been lacking previously. However, the embassy staff were also better prepared this time, so most of the information I brought was superfluous.

After we had registered, Micherline and I were directed inside a classroom to wait. As opposed to previously when there were only two other children, this time there were dozens. There were chairs around the edges of the room and blue and red mats on the floor in the middle. Children and their caretakers were scattered throughout the room. A steady stream of more children and adults entered the room until it was nearly full. Once everyone had gathered, the embassy representatives told us that the children would be leaving at three o'clock, showed us where there was food and water while we waited, and then immediately left us to ourselves.

The other caretakers were all Haitian and didn't speak English. Under normal circumstances my Creole was passable, but with the current stress and emotional fatigue I didn't have the energy to make polite conversation with strangers. Micherline and I sat alone. Micherline was generally a happy little girl, but she was also quiet, and the current circumstances were clearly unnerving to her. Aside from the necessary travel supplies, I had also brought the gifts that her mother had sent her during Micherline's time at the orphanage. Her familiar stuffed bunny and photo album helped calm her nerves, and as we looked at the pictures of her family members I tried to explain that she would be meeting them soon. I got a snack for Micherline, but she seemed to prefer marching her crackers around like little people or stacking them like blocks instead of eating them.

Slowly the time ticked by and, as the designated hour for her departure crept closer, Micherline sensed the shift in the emotional atmosphere. She became clingy and started crying. She refused to wear her shoes and would fuss until I took them off. I could not tell if the shoes were painful or if they represented the unfamiliar to her, as the children were always barefoot in the nurseries. Shoes were usually reserved for special events, and I don't know if Micherline thought that by not wearing the shoes she could prevent whatever strange event was to come. I let her keep the shoes off as long as possible, but when it was time for us to leave, she had to put them on again.

We filed outside with the rest of the children and their caretakers to the buses lined up across the parking lot. I expected more tears and resistance when it was her turn to get on the bus and she was taken from my arms, but Micherline bravely went with the rest of the children. Although she was obviously nervous and confused, she didn't cry or fuss. I was the one in danger of tears. Even though I knew that a caring family was waiting for Micherline on the other side of her journey, it was hard to let go of a frightened little girl who is losing everything she has ever known. Once again, my only comfort was knowing that this was for the best, that soon I would be seeing pictures of Micherline with her family, just as I had with so many of the other children. I had to trust God to watch over Micherline's journey and all the children's transitions to their new homes.

With Micherline's evacuation complete, only fourteen of our original 152 children remained at GLA. Our actual child count was slightly higher than that, with a few staff members' children staying with us and a handful more children who had come in since the earthquake: children brought by parents or relatives unable to provide for them. Whatever the individual circumstances, the result was the same: another child in our care. We were used to the stories—the desperation and need that had led to the necessity of an orphanage in the first place—and we knew that more children would come. We always received more children after hurricanes or flooding, and this disaster was far worse than any we had seen before; hundreds of thousands of children and their families were affected by this tragedy.

Many of the children brought to us were being given up permanently, for eventual adoption when Haiti's government was again functional and processing adoptions. More than the usual percentage, however, were being placed with us for temporary care while their parents got back on their feet after the earthquake. They needed to find a job and a home and a new life for themselves, and they wanted to ensure their child's health and safety while their own situation was still so precarious. We were more than willing to help all the children who came to us, no matter how long their stay or where their eventual home would be.

In the days immediately following the earthquake we had been understaffed, with many of our nannies either unable to find transportation to GLA or needing to stay at home to help out there. Within about a week's time, however, our staff began to return to their normal schedules and, in the weeks immediately following their return, the children were evacuated, country by country. Once the children were gone, it was obvious that we had too many nannies. Even with the new children who arrived, our nurseries were eerily empty and seriously overstaffed. We had expected to receive large numbers of new children who had been displaced or homeless, but since UNICEF had prevented that from happening, we needed to do something about the situation.

By that time, we had nearly as many nannies as children. Rather than increasing the quality of care, though, the nannies became despondent, expecting someone else to change the dirty diapers or comfort a fussing child. The nannies were physically and emotionally exhausted at least as much as we were, and likely more. They were the ones whose country and lives had been most affected by the earthquake. Many of their homes had been damaged or destroyed, and it was their friends, neighbors, and family members who had died. Many of them were in shock or mourning, and it was a struggle for them to do their job properly.

The lowered quality of work was not confined to the nurseries, either. Probably the most distracted staff member was our cook, who had lost eleven family members to the earthquake. He had a hard time concentrating on his task and he often confused his recipes. One night he put a sweet spice in the mashed potatoes, making them taste a bit like pumpkin pie. It was obvious that our staff needed a break.

After careful consideration of who would stay to watch the remaining children, the situation was explained to the staff. We still hoped that more children would come, so their time off would only be temporary. Haitian labor law actually has a clause for just such a situation and, although the law does not require any compensation, GLA chose to pay the laid-off staff members half-pay during their time away. The staff members were grateful for the money, and many of them were pleased to have time off and the opportunity it gave them to spend time with their families, working to put the pieces of their lives back together again.

As for the foreign staff members, our jobs were also largely tied to the children. But now with so few kids—and even fewer of them with adoptive families—our usual jobs were drastically reduced as well. Before the earthquake, I had sent out an average of 120 child updates a month; now I had only fourteen. It became necessary for our jobs, and the focus of our work, to change. While we continued to do what was necessary for the remaining children's adoptions and continued to communicate with their waiting families in France, we also spent much of our time helping with disaster relief.

Within a few weeks of the earthquake, we had received deliveries of all the most essential services: water for drinking and washing, propane for cooking, and diesel for the generator. There was still some uncertainty as to when some of these amenities would be replenished, but what we had received would last us at least a few more weeks. We also continued to receive donations from people who had heard about our need. Their generosity allowed us to not only provide for the children and adults under our roof, but also to share with our neighbors in need and to give staff members supplies for their families.

By the time our staff was back in Haiti after their last evacuation, GLA was overflowing with donations and supplies. Three of the six dorm rooms and the large common room in the staff living quarters were filled with boxes and bags stacked nearly to the ceiling. Even that was not enough space to store everything, and more donations were scattered in other locations throughout GLA's various properties. Many of these supplies were things we needed in the running of an orphanage: diapers, wipes, formula, bottles, and medical supplies. We had also received large quantities of relief items such as tarps and tents, blankets, towels, lanterns and flashlights, soap, and other hygiene products.

We spent much of our time working with the donations and overseeing the relief volunteers who were still in Haiti. After Susan took the most urgently needed items to the nurseries, the rest of the medical and childcare supplies were put into the supply closets and additional overflow was taken to our long-term storage at a different location.

We sorted through the relief supplies, consolidating them into the common room and organizing the items by type—clothes in one pile, blankets in another, and so on. Once we had inventoried the donations received, we began to package them in large garbage bags or plastic storage bins for distribution. We parceled out the items as evenly as we could, making a relief bundle for each of our staff members and additional bundles for others who we knew would need our assistance. Many of the biological parents of children who had been adopted from GLA through the years visited regularly, wanting pictures and updates on their children overseas. Now they came asking for help, and though we could not do much, we did have relief bundles to give them.

Even with all the relief parcels we had given out to our staff, neighbors, and visiting biological families, we still had large amounts of supplies, and we continued receiving more. Many of the most valuable items, such as tents, tarps, lanterns, and small cook stoves were gone, but we had plenty of clothes, towels, blankets, soap, rice, and Dutch military rations. We also began working with political officials in neighboring communities up and down the mountain to distribute bundles to some of those in need there.

Some of the most touching donations we received came in the mail. It was several weeks after the earthquake before we were able to retrieve anything from our missionary mail provider, but once we did, we received several packages sent after the earthquake from people wanting to help. They had sent baby items, medical supplies, spices, simple food staples, and even basic recipes for healthy and filling meals. Not all the packages had return addresses or notes, but those that did told a simple story of learning of our plight and wanting to do something to help. Most of the packages were from the USA and Canada, but one came all the way from Europe. One of our families, whose child had already been evacuated, sent pasta, mushrooms, tuna, and other canned food items—a complete meal! Even more than the blessing of the supplies was the encouragement of knowing the level of love and support we were receiving from around the world. It reminded us that God is faithful and that His provision is certainly not confined to working in the ways we expect.

As we began receiving our mail more regularly again, we received more donations that way, and we also received very special letters from two schools. The first was from a Christian school in England and addressed to the children of Haiti. The youngest schoolchildren had drawn simple pictures, while many of the older ones had written messages of love and hope to the Haitians. The messages were sweet and poignant in their childlike innocence and compassion. The second package we received was from an elementary school class in the US. They had designated us their Valentine's Day project and had filled a box with their love, in the shape of hearts they had cut out of red construction paper.

Nearly a month and a half after the earthquake, the aftershocks began to make a resurgence. Throughout most of January we had experienced regular aftershocks, but by the end of the month the earth's motion seemed to be calming. We began to have a few days together between registered earthquakes (magnitude 4.0 or higher), and even the rocking motion seemed to be decreasing. That changed, however, when six weeks after the first earthquake, most staff members were awakened by magnitude 4.7 aftershocks two nights in a row. Not only that, but there were several smaller aftershocks during the day and the mild vibrations and rocking sensation, which had mostly gone away, returned.

These aftershocks were unnerving, and they brought dizziness, headaches, and the fear that another big earthquake would be coming. A couple of weeks earlier, we had seen a news article where seismologists had analyzed the January 12 earthquake and had predicted the likelihood of another one in the immediate future. Their studies showed that the earthquake had not released as much pressure from the fault line as they would have expected, and thus our chances of having another earthquake, possibly even bigger than the first, were high. They said that, in the next thirty days, there was a ninety percent chance of another earthquake of magnitude 5.0 or higher, a twenty-five percent chance of one 6.0 or higher, and a three percent chance that Haiti would experience another earthquake 7.0 or higher. Normally, that last percentage would have been nearly zero.

As it turned out, none of the aftershocks from that point registered even as high as 5.0, but at the time, we didn't know how things would turn out. All we knew was that we had been through one massive earthquake with more than sixty registered aftershocks and an unknown number of smaller shocks. We were tired, stressed, and emotionally raw. With the return of the aftershocks, some of us also began to struggle with accurately discerning our physical reality. I seemed to feel motion constantly, and I couldn't tell if it was real or imagined. Sometimes people around me felt the motion, too, but other times they didn't. I couldn't be sure if it was my overactive imagination or if I was just more sensitive to the motion than those around me. Since the early days after the first earthquake, we had noticed that some people didn't feel the motion as strongly as others, and that I nearly always felt any motion. However, I also knew that I was feeling paranoid, and I was afraid I was losing my grip on reality.

Eventually, it became necessary for me to take a break from Haiti and the aftershocks and the stress. I had times when I was unable to stay inside, and the smallest things would trigger panic. By this time I was the only staff member who had not been away from Haiti and the constant shaking, and Dixie agreed that I needed the time away. Even though it would be several weeks before I would be able to travel, just knowing that I would get the time away helped calm my mind and emotions. I looked forward to a week at home with stable ground under my feet and no responsibility for anyone other than myself.

Around this time, I accompanied Susan on two trips out of the city to pick up children being transferred to us from a mission in Cazale. The first time we went partway, meeting their mission staff a few miles north of Port-au-Prince, in order to get the sick child to GLA as quickly as possible. The second time it was not quite so urgent, and we went all the way to the more rural area where the mission was situated. Their medical clinic was overwhelmed with caring for earthquake victims, and military doctors who had come to help were seeing patients in camping tents. The whole facility was crowded with patients and activity, and they were clearly doing everything they could for anyone who came to them. They also knew when to ask for help, which was why we were taking some of their most critically ill children. These children needed more intensive medical care, which we were in a much better position to provide.

One of my jobs had always been getting intake pictures of all children upon their arrival at GLA. I had seen many malnourished and emaciated children during my two years there, but never had I seen any who compared to the children who were now coming from Cazale. Valentina was a month old, but she weighed only three and a half pounds, less than she had weighed at birth, which was most likely premature. Donley was much more typical of the malnourished children we saw: a three-day-old baby weighing four pounds.

Clercineau was perhaps the worst of them all, having just passed his first birthday yet weighing only five and a half pounds.

In addition to the children from Cazale, several preemies had been brought to us by their families. We often received premature infants, as we were better equipped to handle them than even most hospitals in Haiti. However, after the earthquake, many more of these tiny babies than normal were brought to us. Presumably, the additional physical and emotional stress of those days caused many women to deliver prematurely. We were thankful we were in a position to help and that the babies were being brought to us.

Unfortunately, one aspect of working with sick and malnourished children in a third world orphanage is that they don't always survive. We had all seen babies die before and, while it wasn't easy, it was sometimes inevitable. The period after the earthquake was especially difficult, though, with nearly as many children dying in the span of a few weeks as had died during all my previous time at GLA. Valentina and Donley both died, as well as two of the preemies who had been brought to us. It was hard on all of us, but especially on Susan and the other nurses who fought so hard and so often, only to lose yet another child. We all needed encouragement—something life-affirming.

Near the end of February, we finally received a few of the children we had been hoping we could help. An orphanage in Port-au-Prince had suffered significant damage to their building in the January 12 earthquake, and their children had been living and sleeping in the outdoor courtyard for the past six weeks. Since this was another orphanage that processed adoptions, no one should object to our caring for the children who, like ours, had been unable to evacuate to join their French families. Thirty-two children were transferred to our care while their adoptions were completed. Many of them had colds and minor infections from spending the chilly nights outside, and a few were more seriously ill and required intensive medical care.

Although they brought our total number of children to a little over fifty and we were still only at about a third of our capacity, it was good to have more children around again. While my job was much reduced, I was once again doing the same things I had done before the earthquake. It was strange at first, to prepare for picture taking and sending updates. Everything I did was filled with memories of the kids who had been there just a few weeks before but were now gone from my life. I missed them, and there was a sharp edge to the joy of photographing the new children. While I was glad to still have a few of the familiar faces I knew and loved, it was also hard to photograph our own French children, knowing they should have been with their families by now.

Progress was slow, but life was beginning to return to the familiar. Every day was another twenty-four hours between us and the earthquake, and twenty-four hours closer to some kind of new normal. As time went on, we gradually stopped marking every Tuesday to count the weeks since the day the earth first shook.

CHAPTER 19

TIME TO BREATHE

There is a time for everything,
and a season for every activity under heaven:
... a time to weep and a time to laugh,
a time to mourn and a time to dance.

~ Ecclesiastes 3:1, 4

WITH THE RETURN TO A more normal routine, we began to experience and recognize the effects of the shock and trauma we had gone through. We were not angels or heroes, in spite of how some in the news media were portraying us. We were ordinary people with no crisis training, trying to survive as best we could in the circumstances thrust upon us. When the earth first shook, all our efforts went into ensuring everyone's continuing survival. At some point, that transitioned into evacuating the children and making sure that everything at the orphanage continued to run smoothly. We were too busy to care for or even notice our own emotional needs.

I remember riding in the car going up the mountain to church, that first Sunday after the earthquake. The last time I had made the same trip had been only a week before, but it now seemed like a lifetime earlier. My first thought was to wish myself back to that easier time, until I realized that meant I would have to relive the horrors of the past few days all over again. My next thought was to wish myself forward—maybe a week, a month, even three months—to a time when things would be easier again. Even that thought was frightening to me, though, because I didn't know that things would in fact be easier. Maybe things would get worse tomorrow, and we would look back with longing at our current struggles.

These were our thoughts, and we lived moment by moment, without taking time to dwell on our emotional trauma. Just making it through each day was exhausting, and we had no extra energy to process our struggles or even care about what others thought of us. Many of us put down the masks we often wore and our true emotions came much closer to the surface. It was too tiring to pretend that everything was all right, and we were much more transparent about our thoughts and fears when we communicated with our friends and supporters back home. Even so, we didn't want to cause them excessive worry when there was nothing they could do to change our situation, so we did withhold some of our bleakest thoughts and most dire circumstances. We didn't even share them with one another: as if we could prevent the bad things we feared, simply by keeping silent. Those thoughts that we were keeping inside added to our emotional strain.

Once our situation began to calm, however, all those emotions and fears started surfacing inside of us, and we realized that we were suffering from post-traumatic stress. We didn't know how to cope with our new lives, but the old ones were now gone forever. Even as our circumstances and surroundings returned to a more normal routine, it became obvious that we had changed. We had lost our innocence, our sense of security. Never again would we believe that disaster could not strike us. Never again would we be able to wholly embrace the lie that we were in control of our lives.

The possibility of another earthquake was still very real to all of us in those days. We never entered a room, especially some place new or unfamiliar, without immediately locating the nearest exit. Many of us learned to position ourselves with easy access to the door, so that we could get out quickly, should that be necessary. Even when showering, on the bottom floor of the dorm where I lived, I made sure that all doors were unlocked and my towel was easily accessible, in case I needed to evacuate in the middle of my shower.

The ground was still rumbling; our bodies were still on high alert in a constant fight-or-flight mode. They had been that way for a long time, and it would take even longer to stop that reflex. One therapist who visited during that time explained that it was not only our bodies as a whole that had experienced and remembered the trauma, but each individual cell within us. That was why sometimes we felt panic, even when our rational brain told us that it was only the heavy water truck causing the rumbling of the earth.

We were constantly discovering new triggers for our fears: things we had not realized or expected. But we were learning that the effects of a trauma such as we had experienced are varied and unpredictable. When I went to delete old text messages off my cell phone for the first time after the earthquake, I felt an irrational panic. I had not even consciously remembered that that's what I had been doing when the earthquake started, but some part of my body knew and was somehow afraid that was what had triggered the disaster.

In addition to all that we had been through physically and emotionally with the earthquake, we were also struggling with the sorrow and loss of our children. Our children didn't die in the earthquake, but in many ways our loss was similar. We had the assurance that our children were still alive and walking around somewhere on earth, but we didn't know exactly where that somewhere was, and in many cases the separation from them was just as permanent as if they had died. Our ultimate goal had always been to let these children go when they joined their forever families, but the suddenness of their departure, and our ongoing needs had prevented us from processing everything that had happened. With nothing urgently requiring our attention anymore, the grief now struck us full force. It was necessary for us to acknowledge our loss so that we could move on with our lives as emotionally healthy as possible. By the end of February, I was starting to see the light, so to speak. I could not yet see the end of the tunnel of our circumstances, but at least I once again had a little hope.

As strange as it may seem, another challenge we faced was trying to figure out how to move on with our lives. For several weeks, we had not known one day of the week from the next. There had been no such thing as regular work hours or weekends. When things began to slow down again, at least to the point where we didn't have to be working constantly, it was actually a struggle to accept that this was okay. The first Saturday that I had a few hours to myself, I spent them alone on the balcony, reading and trying to relax. My body and mind had a hard time slowing down enough to rest, though, as they had become so used to constantly being engaged, jumping from one task to the next. It didn't seem right that I could simply sit for even a few hours without there being something that required my immediate attention.

I also remember the first time I noticed new flowers blooming. They signified the passing of time, the changing of seasons. It didn't feel right, somehow, that time should be moving on so heartlessly when so many were still suffering. It reminded me of the time several years earlier when my grandmother had died, and the strange feeling that came over me as I stepped outside the hospital and into the brilliant sunshine. It seems wrong for life and beauty and love to continue when we are in great pain.

In spite of our personal struggles, we could not help but acknowledge the miracles that had occurred in the middle of the tragedy, and we now had time to appreciate them more fully. An amazing thing about being in the middle of a disaster is the million little things that bring you hope. God is always at work, but much of what He is doing is behind the scenes, and so is never known or understood. When the world is falling apart around you, however, the hand of God can be more clearly seen putting the pieces back together. So often we only live within the realm of our natural expectations, and we define what is possible by our own abilities. We may pray for God to do big things, but so rarely do we see these prayers answered that we often don't truly believe He will. We go through so many disappointments that eventually we are afraid to fully trust Him.

I think the real problem is our very limited perspective. God is working in us, through us, and around us all the time to accomplish

His purposes. Not only are these purposes much bigger than we could ever imagine, but He works in ways that are not what we would expect. Nor would we always approve of His methods, if He asked our opinions! God's ultimate goal and plan in our lives, in any situation, is not to seek our comfort and happiness; He has nobler goals and plans. The stories of faith and hope that are born in tragedy are the ones that capture people's attention. When you see and experience the miracles that God works in the midst of suffering and what was intended for evil, it is a beautiful thing. And then no one but God can receive the glory.

Our most obvious miracle was the unification of our children with their adoptive families. At the time of the earthquake, the normal course of a Haitian adoption took eighteen to thirty months, in addition to the time the family spent preparing their paperwork and the wait until they were matched with a child in the orphanage. Most of our children had still been months away from going home to their forever families, and many had been a year or more away from that time. Yet by the end of January, less than three weeks after the earthquake, over ninety percent of our children were safely home with their families. Just a few weeks earlier, no one would have believed that was possible.

We also learned to depend on God in a whole new way, and He continually proved Himself faithful. It was in our desperation, so foreign to most of us from the Western world, that our lives came closest to the daily experience of millions around the world: never knowing where our next meal would come from, and lacking the supplies and the ability to ensure the safety of those we loved. We were required to rely wholly on God, and that was foreign to us. His ways were often not predictable, but our needs were always met. We saw His promises in the scriptures lived out before our eyes. Learning to trust Him was not always easy, but it was good. He truly was our solid rock in a time when even the ground beneath us was not.

We were thankful for family and friends who were a faithful support to us during that time. Besides praying for us, many offered encouragement and spoke God's truths to us. We were always willing to listen to those who were walking through this valley with us, even if from afar. What was not always helpful were the words of those who showed they didn't truly understand our situation. Platitudes and trite phrases were often hurtful, even when kindly intended. Even worse were those who felt there was no reason for our grief. They rebuked us for our lack of joy and exhorted us to sing praises and celebrate before the Lord. Fortunately, those people were the minority in our lives, but they did add to our pain and confusion.

We found comfort in the stories of Job and Joseph and others in the Bible who had suffered circumstances outside their control. They were our models; they grieved and cried out their pain, but they remained faithful to God, trusting Him for their deliverance. Not only that, but they came out on the other side stronger for what they had been through. That was what we hoped to be said about our own lives, since we found ourselves in tragic circumstances similar to theirs.

It was not only in our lives that God was working; He was working throughout Port-au-Prince. Many of the Haitians turned or returned to God, and a revival swept through the people. In the time immediately following the earthquake, the visible presence of voudou disappeared, and people stood in the streets singing praises to God. Exactly one month after the earthquake was the start of Kanaval, which is the Haitian Mardi Gras. Along with the Mardi Gras activities one might expect, it is typically an extremely active time for voudou. Instead of the traditional Kanaval celebrations, though, the president declared February 12, 2010, an official day of remembrance. Churches and religious leaders asked the Haitian people to spend that weekend in a time of prayer and fasting for the nation, which they did with typical exuberance. Our own nannies and staff joined their countrymen, praising the true God and begging for His help to rebuild their nation and their lives. In fact, on the morning of February 12, I awoke to the sound of praise songs being sung in the courtyard just outside my room. God used the tragedy to draw many people to Himself.

During that time, I also learned to adjust my own thinking and how I determine whether circumstances are positive or negative. It reminded me of a folk tale I had heard several years earlier, of a man whose son experienced a string of positive and negative events. The man's neighbor qualified each event as good or bad, but the man replied after each one that only time would tell whether what had happened was really good or bad. And in fact, each situation that seemed to be good led directly to something that seemed to be bad, which led to something that seemed to be good, and so on. That was how I felt during that time, because several things that I had thought annoyances at the time turned out to be for the best, in light of the earthquake.

The first of these events was a decision that an adoption judge had made the summer before. He started requiring all adoptive families to come to Haiti, meet their child, and sign additional paperwork before he would approve their adoptions. For those of us at GLA and for most of the adoptive families, this was a major nuisance, as dozens of families' adoptions were stalled until this requirement was met. For the families, it required an immediate trip to Haiti and an extra financial burden in an already expensive adoption process. From GLA's perspective, it meant coordinating travel and housing arrangements for more than one hundred families, all needing to come as soon as possible.

In addition, we usually discouraged families from temporarily visiting their children before the adoption was complete, because we didn't want to cause the children any emotional harm. Every one of the children in our care had been abandoned at least once, and we didn't want to take the chance that they would associate their future parents with feelings of abandonment.

Initially we had tried to fight the judge's decision, but it was a futile battle, and we set about the task of completing this extra step in the adoption process. It was a crazy time, but somehow we made it through the worst of it. One thing we never expected was that we would one day be thankful for the judge's decision.

Once we started evacuating children in January, however, we were relieved that so many parents had made that trip. Not only had we met the parents who would be taking the children, but the children themselves had met their parents, and within the past six months. The older kids especially had memories of time spent with their visiting parents, had seen pictures of their future homes, and had learned a little of what their new lives would be. They had been telling and retelling these stories to their friends, and the memories were fresh in their minds. Even the younger children had some memory and sense of their time with their parents, which we trusted would bring recognition and a sense of safety and security when they met them again; we were not sending them off to total strangers.

Those parents' visits had also allowed them the opportunity to come to Haiti, to see and experience a little bit of their children's native culture. If we had had our way, they would not have come until the completion of their adoptions, and in this case that would have been too late. Now they would be able to answer at least some of the questions their children would one day ask about their country of birth.

Another blessing in disguise was personal. When I returned to Haiti after spending Christmas with my family, the airline lost my luggage. This was the first time that had happened to me in six years of travelling back and forth to Haiti, and I had known for some time that the law of averages would catch up to me. Still, I was not happy that it happened just then, especially since I had brought with me some of the supplies I needed to take the children's pictures that month.

I arrived on Monday—eight days before the earthquake—and I was told my bags would come in later the same day. Instead, they came on Wednesday. I had planned on taking the children's pictures immediately upon my return, but without the background I would use for the photos, I was forced to wait. Much of the rest of my job required those pictures to be taken first, so there was little work I could do. I therefore was free to spend more time than normal with the children, playing with them in the nurseries and on the balcony. When my luggage did finally arrive, I was able to take all the photographs, seeing and spending at least a few minutes with every child in the orphanage. I finished the last of the photographs less than an hour and a half before the ground shook.

Now that the evacuations were over and life was again calmer, I still had those final photographs of the children. I had not sent them out in monthly updates, since the children were already at home. Now, I edited the pictures for each child's photo CD: a compilation of all our photographs of that child since their arrival at GLA. It was an opportunity for me to remember each one and what he or she meant to me. Many times I wished that I could reach through my computer screen and hold those dear children once more. I could not do that, but at least I could say good-bye in my own way and find some closure to our relationship.

Because of the hurry and chaos of the evacuations, only the few most important legal documents had been sent along with the children. Now we were collecting the rest of the information and paperwork we had, so the families would have the completed files. It would still be several weeks or more, however, before the files were collected and we found a way to transport them to the countries where they needed to go, but there was some information the families needed immediately. I spent a few days scanning the children's vaccine records and emailing them to the families, since the children were seeing doctors who had no clue about their medical history. We were also receiving emails from the families, asking about their children's habits and health. Because of the nature of the transition, we had not been able to pass along as much information as we normally would have, so now we did our best by email.

Another part of my job, in those days after evacuation, was to package the gifts the children's parents had sent them while they were with us . We had volunteers travelling to the different countries who offered to transport as many of those gifts as possible. I sorted through the gifts, making sure the most important and sentimental things were returned to the children and their families.

Though the earthquake experience was not yet over—and in some ways it would always be with us—its immediate effects were winding down. We were closing the children's files and moving on to the next stage of life, both as individuals and as an organization. Media attention had long since moved off of Haiti's earthquake, and we sensed the shift in our own lives as well, even though we didn't yet know what was next or how to rebuild our lives.

It was mid-March when I first left Haiti for what I called my sanity break. I had not been to the airport in nearly two months. I did see some encouraging progress in the clean-up process, though the work still needing to be done was daunting. Men were knocking down buildings that were cracked and partially collapsed. Typical of Haiti, everything was being done by hand, workers using sledgehammers to break cement and concrete away from the rebar. Many side roads were blocked off, since countless homeless Haitians had set up camp and were living in tents and under tarps in the streets. Any park or other open area was similarly populated, and these camps felt more permanent than the ones I had seen on my first trip to the airport. This was especially concerning since rainy season was now only a few weeks away.

One of the things I was most worried about was my flight, because in recent weeks I had been prone to claustrophobia and being closed in with no way of escape. I was also concerned about possible turbulence, because several coworkers had told me it had reminded them of the earthquake. Takeoff did feel very much like an earthquake—with its shaking, the loud noise, the rattling of windows—and it was very frightening, but I didn't have a problem with turbulence. I was pleasantly surprised at this, though confused, because I was usually sensitive to even the smallest motions. However, that changed when the plane experienced turbulence while I was standing in the aisle waiting for the bathroom. Not only was it deeply disconcerting, but I felt nauseous, and I feared I might be sick. After a moment, I realized that my reaction was because of the difference in the direction of the motion. Most of my co-workers' desks were situated so that they felt the earthquake side-to-side, while for me it had been front-to-back. When I sat in the airplane's seat I felt a side-to-side motion, which did not trigger strong earthquake associations for me. When I was standing, however, I was facing the side of the plane and the turbulence thus shook me front-to-back. That was the earthquake motion I was familiar with, and it terrified me.

After a week spent at home, away from the intensity of constant stress and fear, I returned to Haiti in time for the arrival of one of our French mothers. France had ultimately decided against evacuating the children, requiring them to remain in Haiti until their adoptions were legally complete. Since theirs were the only children still in Haiti, those files were being expedited, and now Nadége was ready to go home.

Nadége had always been a special child to those of us at GLA, having been brought to us when she was only two weeks old. She had been small and fragile, needing extra love and attention. Susan had arrived at GLA shortly after Nadége had and, at Dixie's request, had taken her into her own room to provide the intensive care and attention Nadége needed. She had thrived with the extra personal care and love she received, and when she returned to the nursery several weeks later, Nadége was healthy and happy.

That had been seventeen months before the earthquake, and Nadége had grown into a lively, spirited little girl. She still loved attention, of which she received plenty, and she knew her own mind. She was one of the few children who picked her own clothes for photo day, since she knew what she wanted to wear and would make sure that you knew as well. As a true French child, she did have a good sense of style, though she was still well under two years old! Nadége was perpetually happy; she knew she was loved, and she loved us back. Though she did well at GLA, we all knew that she would thrive even more once she was in her own family, where she would get even more of the individual love and attention she so craved.

Nadége's French mother, Catherine, was also very special to us, having previously been a volunteer at GLA. She was universally loved, and everyone was excited when we learned that she would be the mother of our precious Nadége.

Catherine was the first parent to come to GLA in the usual way since the earthquake, and we greeted her joyfully. She had been with us only a few months before, due to the judge's decree, and Catherine and Nadége's reunion was everything we could have hoped for. Once again a family was brought together in the comfort of the child's own surroundings. They had the time to bond in the child's comfort zone, surrounded by the love and support of friends. When they left a few days later, it was not with the bittersweet emotions we had felt in the mass boarding of our children onto planes. This time we were able to wave good-bye with peace in our hearts.

There was something profoundly healing in seeing things return to the way they had been, in watching a mother and child meet and leave together. We began to believe that there was hope again, that the way of life we had known was not gone forever. We would not always live in the shadow of January 12, 2010.

EPILOGUE

IN MAY 2010, FOUR MONTHS after the earthquake and two years after I had arrived at God's Littlest Angels, I moved back to the United States. I had sensed that my time in Haiti was nearing its completion when I returned to GLA after the Christmas holidays, though I had no idea when I would leave or what the events of my final months in Haiti would be. The earthquake pushed all thoughts of leaving out of my head, but once the challenges of the immediate aftermath were over and the children evacuated, there was no longer a reason for me to stay. More children were coming to the orphanage, but our numbers were still low. Most of the children I had known were gone, and I felt God leading me in another direction. I would go home, and someone else could start fresh with the new kids who were arriving.

When I returned home, many well-intentioned but uninformed people asked questions about me and Haiti, assuming that the answers were obvious. They expected to hear that I was thankful to be home and out of Haiti. They wanted me to tell them that Port-au-Prince had recovered from the earthquake and was back to "normal," or at least well on its way to being so. I could do neither. The truth was that I missed Haiti and my friends there. And the process of rebuilding the city and the nation had barely begun. Even now, several years later, Haitians are displaced and living in tents, and the city bears the scars of that long-ago Tuesday afternoon.

Haiti will never be what it was before; neither will anyone who lived through this experience. Hopefully the nation and all of us will be stronger because of it, but the earthquake has left its mark. This is no fairy tale with a "happily ever after" ending. Though the evacuations were happy endings to the children's time at the orphanage, as is usually the case, those endings were really only the beginning of the rest of their lives.

Parents had to learn how to be mothers and fathers for the first time, or all over again with new children. Siblings had to adjust to changes in their families now that new brothers or sisters had arrived. Haitian children had to adapt to all that was new in their lives—family, language, country, culture, food, weather, and so much more. Parents struggled with how to help their traumatized children, hoping that love and grace would help them through. Individuals began the painful and wonderful process of becoming families.

Adoption is beautiful, but it can be challenging as well. Even under the best of circumstances, the children have faced at least the one loss that brought them to the orphanage, but these children had faced the additional traumas of the earthquake and sudden evacuation. They now carried that pain inside of them, as well as their grief at the loss of home and everything else they had known. Since most of them lacked the words or the ability to express these feelings, their emotions came out in other ways. Some tested boundaries or reacted out of proportion to what was appropriate for the situation. Others developed new fears: of loud noises, or the dark, or unexpected motion, like driving over railroad tracks or riding in an elevator. It was a difficult transition, and different for each family and situation, but the parents continued to show their love to their children, and the children began to trust these new adults in their world as parents. Family bonds were formed.

Others longed to know the struggles of a new family. Most of our children were evacuated, but not all. The French government continued to insist that the children complete the normal process of adoption before they could come home to France. It was not until December 2010 that a cholera outbreak in Haiti finally prompted them to evacuate all remaining children. The last of the children to go home was actually an American who had been unable to evacuate with the others due to a last-minute change in his paperwork. He faced one obstacle after another before he was able to join his family at last, his adoption finally completed more than three years after the earthquake.

In addition to the blessing of having a family, the evacuations likely saved the lives of several of our children:

Roselaure was diagnosed with bacterial meningitis and given only a slim chance for a full recovery. After more than a month in the hospital, though, she went home to her parents and her brother Steevenson, a healthy and vibrant little girl.

Lovely was also hospitalized in Miami with a bacterial infection in her bloodstream, a situation that would have been critical in Haiti.

Jephté's seizures had been worsening in Haiti, and our nurses were losing the battle to keep them under control.

Atlanta was still fragile from her malnutrition. We were not equipped to deal with the extent of her needs, especially through our post-quake challenges.

Marquelove made it to Michigan before she was hospitalized, but she faced dehydration, pneumonia, and an ear infection.

Many others were sick and so visited the doctor soon after arriving home. We do not know what would have happened with any of these children had they stayed in Haiti, but it is probable that going home saved at least some of their lives.

In spite of the miracles that we experienced, the earthquake was a terrible tragedy, especially for the Haitian people. Haiti had nothing, yet somehow they still lost everything. Like many others, I have questioned why God allowed the earthquake. I have struggled with His lack of intervention to heal so many of the world's abuses. The problem of evil is very real, very difficult, and something that everyone responds to differently at different times and situations.

For me, in this instance, it comes down to perspective. I no longer ask why God allowed a destructive earthquake in a nation that was poorly equipped to survive everyday life, much less a massive disaster. I marvel that He so often holds the tectonic plates together and keeps the world from breaking into millions of pieces.

Though I do not know God's purpose in the earthquake and in the lives of others, I know that I have learned far more about the hugeness of God through the earthquake experience than I ever could have imagined in a lifetime of comfortable existence. Because I have come out on the other side, I can see that I am stronger than I ever knew, or could have known, without this experience. God has shown me that He is as faithful to me today as He was to Abraham,

David, and the others whose stories are in the Bible. I would not have chosen this experience, but looking back, I would not change it.

One of the most comforting passages to me in the months after the earthquake was 1 Kings 19:11–13a:

> The LORD said, "Go out and stand on the mountain in the presence of the LORD, for the LORD is about to pass by." Then a great and powerful wind tore the mountains apart and shattered the rocks before the LORD, but the LORD was not in the wind. After the wind there was an earthquake, but the LORD was not in the earthquake. After the earthquake came a fire, but the LORD was not in the fire. And after the fire came a gentle whisper. When Elijah heard it, he pulled his cloak over his face and went out and stood at the mouth of the cave.

God was not in the earthquake: He was in the peace that came after all the noise and chaos.

The aftermath of the Haiti earthquake was a time when we saw God work in mighty and powerful ways. Miraculous ways. More often, though, He speaks in a gentle whisper.

For more information about
Melanie Wright Zeeb
&
Beauty from Ashes
please visit:

MelanieZeeb.com
MelanieWrite.pgj@gmail.com
@MelZeeb
facebook.com/AuthorMelanieZeeb

For more information about
AMBASSADOR INTERNATIONAL
please visit:

www.ambassador-international.com
@AmbassadorIntl
www.facebook.com/AmbassadorIntl